The Renegade Writer

Marion Street Press, Inc.

The Renegade Writer

A Totally Unconventional Guide to Freelance Writing Success

By Linda Formichelli and Diana Burrell

Marion Street Press, Inc.

"A fresh, and dare I say exciting, view of how to run a successful freelance writing business, by writers who know. Recommended reading for every writer who wants to increase sales, get published, and make more money."

- *Bob Bly*
Author of Secrets of a Freelance Writer

"What a load off of writers' shoulders: You can break the rules and be successful! The authors are eminent professionals who lead by example. You, too, can be a bold, brazen, renegade writer by learning what really works in the modern publishing world. The meek may inherit the Earth, but they don't land writing assignments. Renegade writers do. Highly recommended."

- *Jenna Glatzer*
Editor-in-Chief, absolutewrite.com
Author of The More Than Any Human Being Needs To Know About Freelance Writing Workbook

"Whether you're an experienced pro or a young writer newly embarking on a freelance career, *The Renegade Writer* delivers no-nonsense tips and sure-fire techniques to help you achieve freelance success. Thanks to Linda and Diana, your dreams of freelance fame, fortune and fun are now within your grasp."

- *Nancy Flynn*
Author of The $100,000 Writer

"Break the rules and get rich is the message of this smart, witty, and well-researched road map to success. Whether you're a freelancer who is trying to break into print, crack bigger and better markets, or take your writing to the next level, *The Renegade Writer* has the advice you need, in a lively, reader-friendly format that will keep you turning the pages for more."

- Lisa Collier Cool
National Magazine Award winner and best-selling author of How to Write Irresistible Query Letters

"Forget what you think you know about freelancing. In *The Renegade Writer*, Linda and Diana turn all of those so-called rules upside down and in doing so, show how you can get your work published, make more money, and succeed as a freelance writer. Filled with practical tips and hundreds of real-life examples, both beginning and experienced writers will find a wealth of information and useful ideas in this book."

- Kelly James-Enger
Author of Ready, Aim, Specialize!

"I'm actually MAD at you because I am reading the book when I should be working, it's that good."

- Bob Bly
Author of Secrets of a Freelance Writer

Library of Congress Cataloging-in-Publication Data

Formichelli, Linda, 1969-
  The renegade writer : a totally unconventional guide to
freelance
writing success / by Linda Formichelli and Diana Burrell.
     p. cm.
Includes bibliographical references and index.
  ISBN 0-9665176-8-7
  1. Journalism--Authorship. 2. Feature writing. I. Burrell,
Diana,
1964- II. Title.
  PN147.F65 2003
  808'.06607--dc21

                                          2003011893

Cover design by Anne Locascio

ISBN 0-9665176-8-7
Printed in U.S.A.
Printing 10 9 8 7 6 5 4 3 2 1

Marion Street Press, Inc.
PO Box 2249
Oak Park, IL 60303
866-443-7987
www.marionstreetpress.com

Join the Club!

The Renegade Writer Club is a great way to network with other freelancers who are willing to break the rules. Membership is free, and you get a monthly email newsletter packed with rule-breaking ideas, info about local Renegade Writer groups, discounts on select writing books, a Renegade Writer bumper sticker, and more! Join today at www.marionstreetpress.com.

Contents

Putting Pen to Paper
Yes, Renegade Writers Even Break Grammar Rules!
127

Getting the Green
Don't Be Shy When It Comes Time To Collect
143

The Renegade Attitude
Your Success Often Depends On Your Mindset
155

Thriving, Not Just Surviving
Don't Settle For Anything Less Than Reaching The Top
167

Appendices

Diana's Acknowledgments

My parents nurtured my need to write from the time I could hold a pencil, and they still brag about my first literary achievement, "Glinda and the Golden Pin" (age 6). My father John Burrell and stepmother Jan are the first down at the newsstand to read my articles. My mother Agnes Maloney and stepfather Jim generously provided me with a first-rate education, and they've never complained about me squandering it on freelancing. Thank you – I couldn't have better parents and stepparents.

Many thanks to the "jugglers" at FLX who gave me great advice for balancing work and family. Dear friends Kate Stiffle and Sean Cronin deserve big hugs. They let me whine and kvetch to my heart's content, and they still return my phone calls. A special thanks to the incredible Alison Stein Wellner, who's not quoted in here, but should be!

I can't mention my husband's name in print (besides, he knows who he is), but he was a great help through the whole process of writing this book – from brainstorming and rescuing my iMac from certain destruction, to babysitting and letting me take frequent "naplets." He has always been my #1 fan. And while our son, Oliver, didn't provide much direct help with this book, he was a great motivator for it. Thanks to my main squeezes. I love you both.

Most of all, thanks to my co-author and friend, Linda, a/k/a L-stud. I've learned a lot from you – everything from how to break into the big leagues to how to stick the word "ass" into every chapter – you rock!

Linda's Acknowledgments

Not only is my husband W. Eric Martin a babelicious freelance writer, but he also did a super job of editing the manuscript before we turned it in. If it weren't for him, we would've used the word "just" 87 times. Glory be to Eric!

My parents, Anthony and Janet Formichelli, deserve thanks for always encouraging my writing habit, even when my most impressive clip was from *The Association of KFC Franchisees Quarterly* magazine. This book was a true family affair; my mom spent six hours on Christmas Day proofreading the manuscript and my brother, Chris Formichelli, designed our awesome Web site. Thank you!

A special thanks to Diana, the best co-author a girl could wish for. Our writing styles and senses of humor are so similar that when I read this book, I often can't remember who wrote what (although I'm pretty sure Diana was responsible for all occurrences of the word "ass").

We'd both like to thank the many editors and experts who generously shared their expertise with us. In no particular order, there's Ken Gordon, Denise Foley, Susan Pennell, Dick Baumer, Arnold Howard, Elisa Bosley, Nancy LaPatourel, Cindy Sweeney, Melanie Fogel, Daniel Kehrer, Anne M. Russell, Brian Alm, Suma CM, Angela Giles Klocke, Dian Killian, Brett Harvey, James MacKinnon, Rebecca Rolfes, Maggie Bonham, Howard Faulkner, Ph.D., Jeremy White, Tom Bivins, Karen Axelton, and Kim Lisi. An extra special thanks to publisher extraordinaire Ed Avis and cover designer Anne Locascio for turning *The Renegade Writer* into a reality.

And a very special thank you to all the renegade writers we interviewed for this book (See Appendix 13, p. 197).

Introduction

Maybe the dream started in the eighth grade when you wrote a controversial article about the new school dress code: Replacing "Boy Toy"- emblazoned T-shirts with button-down Oxfords surely doomed you to remain "like a virgin" for the rest of your life. You eagerly interviewed friends, teachers, and even a few parents, then jotted off a heartfelt thousand words about why this idiotic dress code gagged you with a spoon. When the article appeared in the paper, you were praised by your friends for espousing an opinion that was unpopular with the teachers, and by your English teacher for expressing teenage angst so eloquently. Flush with pride, you may have thought, "Gee, I could make a living at this someday. I may even become famous! Madonna, watch out!"

Chances are, you were praised somewhere along the line for your writing efforts, and maybe you took that talent to law school or an advertising agency. But every time you pick up an issue of *Redbook* or *National Geographic Traveler* or even *Modern Reprographics*, a prick of jealousy stabs you as you skim the bylines of writers who get paid to write about how to jazz up your sex life or restaurants in Venice or new developments in vegetable-based inks. And they do all this from a home office, while you have to suffer annoying co-workers and cranky clients from your corporate cubicle. You're making a living, but is it the living you dreamed of back in junior high?

Or perhaps you've already shucked the corporate chains for a life of freelance writing. You're mailing out those one-page query letters as every writing book and magazine instructs you to do.

Oh, yeah, with the self-addressed, stamped envelope (SASE) enclosed – can't forget that. Funny thing is, you're getting nada in return – not even your SASE. Or maybe you've been plugging along for a couple of years, making a decent amount of money, but feel you still haven't realized your initial inspiration: You can't seem to crack a dream magazine, or you feel like you've been pegged as a technology writer when you'd rather be writing about human relationships.

Whether you're a seasoned freelancer or a wannabe writer, it's easy to believe the rumors, myths, and misconceptions about freelance writing. These bugaboos abound because freelancers work largely on their own, isolated from other writers, so they have no real-life examples to learn from. But if you were to share office space with a group of professional magazine writers and observe them for weeks on end *à la* Jane Goodall, we guarantee that they'd shatter most every myth about freelancing you carry around in that fertile imagination of yours. Moreover, the world has changed, but the good people writing books on how to freelance seem not to have noticed this because they still urge writers to send SASEs with their submissions (what, haven't they heard of e-mail?) or tell writers to cop a servile attitude around editors.

Don't get us wrong – we adore all the books about writing on our office shelves. Really. The two of us probably own enough of these tomes to span the distance between our houses, and have studied a few of them better than any book we studied in college. The funny thing is, though, we've found that the rules in these books don't bring us the fame, the fortune, or at least the 1099s that we so desire.

And yet, here we are, asking you to read *our* writing book and bow in obeisance to our awesome observations – are we shameless hypocrites or what? Well, why don't you listen to our stories?

Introduction

Diana's Story

I didn't set out to be a magazine writer. No, for most of my life, my writerly goal was much more lofty: I wanted to be a novelist. I wanted to be a female J. D. Salinger, a chronicler of youthful angst, but Douglas Coupland beat me to that (except for the female part). Then I toyed with short fiction, and actually had a story published in my college's literary magazine. But short fiction won't get you rich, and soon my aspirations for fame had transformed into a yearning for A) a satisfying career that would B) meet or exceed my current standard of living.

With my bachelor's degree in American studies relegated to a back drawer, I spent 10 years in product marketing and advertising for several companies. I went through staff downsizings, computer upgrades, and mid-year reviews with Dilberty bosses — enough so that my natural sense of curiosity about the world nearly shriveled up and died. Yes, I was making good money and traveling to places like Fayetteville, Arkansas (really, I enjoyed it), but I didn't have time to eat right or exercise. When I found time to mull over the path my life had taken, I wondered what had happened to the girl who'd listed "writer" as her goal under her high school yearbook picture.

A former boyfriend and I used to visit friends of his who had a summer place in the Hamptons, and as the fates would have it, one of them was a senior editor at a women's magazine in New York. One day while lounging poolside, I asked her about her job, and specifically about writing. She gave me a crash course in the difference between a great freelancer and an editor's nightmare. She confirmed, for example, that most of the proposals landing on her desk were either not targeted to her magazine or poorly written. And the stuff that set the pros apart — writing well, making deadlines, being pleasant to deal with — were things I knew I could do with my eyes closed. By the end of the conversation, wheels were turning in my head. Based on what she'd said, I knew freelance writing was a career in which I could succeed, even thrive.

I wish I could report that I marched back to my job in Connecticut, promptly quit, and started cashing huge checks from Condé Nast. But no, I made the mistake a lot of beginning freelancers and wannabes make – I denied the siren's song. I changed jobs, hoping that I'd finally find fulfillment in a cubicle. (Nope. Nope. And nope. That's how many times I switched jobs before summoning the courage to go freelance.) I even thought about entering a full-time graduate program in English literature.

The only thing that did pan out were classes in magazine writing and editing – but not for the reasons you might suspect. In one of them, I happened to befriend a classmate who was an assistant editor at the glossy, upscale *Connecticut Magazine*, which published features about interesting people, events, and places in the Nutmeg State. Around that time, I started writing a romance novel and attending local Romance Writers of America meetings. The women who attended these meetings, both published authors and wannabes, were a quirky, interesting bunch – perfect candidates for a profile. So I asked my new friend if I could send her a proposal, she said okay, and I fired off two single-spaced pages packed full of juicy details that I knew she couldn't resist. I was so confident she'd buy it, I even told the romance writers that the assignment was in the bag. (I considered this a positive mental attitude, not lying.)

Lucky for me, the assignment came through, so I didn't have to skulk back to the romance writers and tell them the truth. The writing and editing process with the magazine went well and as I worked at my computer, I found myself yearning to work like this full-time. Still, I hung back from sending out more proposals and continued to toil away in my latest marketing management job, complete with a mentally unstable boss and cutthroat cube jockeys.

That New York magazine editor may have planted the freelancing seed in my head, but my boyfriend (now husband) gets full credit for kindling the fire under my butt. He convinced me to quit my job, move in with him up in Boston, and use some of my savings to jumpstart my new career. Like a doofus, I diddled the

Introduction

opportunity away, taking full-time jobs when money got uncomfortably low — but I did flex my freelancing muscles more and more: I became a freelance features correspondent for a chain of local newspapers and I sold my first article to a national consumer magazine, *Walking*.

I made the final leap right before our wedding. You see, I was working in a huge multinational company as a tech writer for a psycho boss who could not write. Seriously. She was just really good at being paranoid and screaming at those who *could* write. One day she publicly berated me for looking off into space. (I was *thinking*, an activity that was alien to her.) When I called my fiancé at lunchtime and told him what happened, he said, "If you don't quit today, I will come over there and quit for you." Now, my husband is one of those guys who says what he means and means what he says; he wasn't kidding. I could hear the car keys jingling in his hand. And that's when it finally hit me: I was tired of not being happy with the work I was doing. I went back to my office, wrote up a resignation letter, walked into the boss's office and gave her my two weeks. (Obviously, knowing that my husband-to-be was going to be my sugar daddy for a few months made this a bit easier — and more enjoyable!)

There's an old saying, "A bad day fishing beats a good day at work." That's how I feel about freelancing: rejection letters, rewrites, slow payments … I wouldn't trade them for anything (well, except for more acceptances, no rewrites, and direct deposit). We've got health insurance, saved for retirement, bought a house, and taken excellent vacations, so I don't buy the whole "starving freelancer" myth. (And before you assume my husband's got some high-paying corporate job, let me tell you that he's an independent consultant, as reliant upon the market and self-motivation as any freelance writer.)

These days, with an active toddler running in and out of my office, I'm happier than ever to have the job I have. My hours are flexible, and if I want to blow off an afternoon and take my son to the zoo, I can. When he was born, I cut back on my work hours. As he gets older, I'll add more hours to increase my income. And I know that the techniques I've used in the past – the ones you'll read about in this book – will continue to serve me well.

Linda's Story

I always wanted to be a writer, and like Diana, it was fiction that I dreamed of. When I was in first grade, I wrote my first poem, which I still remember:

> There once was a mouse
> Who lived in my house
> And when he squeaked
> I often peeked
> To see what he was doing
> Didn't say please
> Just stole the cheese
> And that's what he was chewing.

Hey, give me a break – I was six years old!

In high school, I wrote all sorts of teenage-angsty stories and poems, two of which were printed in the high school literary magazine: A poem about a girl who was so smart that her head exploded, and a short story about a psychology student who suffered from various maladies as he wrote about them on his final exam.

In college, I decided to take a different track and ended up majoring in Russian and minoring in German, hoping to become a translator. (This was during the Cold War, you see.) I ended up with a master's degree in Slavic linguistics, although I had no idea what to do with such knowledge. In the meantime, the creative writing fell by the wayside.

After grad school, I got it into my head to go into publishing, so I went on informational interviews at several publishing companies. I didn't like what I learned about the business, but I thought the experience would make a great article. I read *Queries and Submissions* by Thomas Clark, wrote up my first query, bought a copy of *Writer's Market*, picked out a few career magazines, and sent the queries off to the pubs. (Simultaneous submissions *and* querying magazines I wasn't familiar with – see, I'm a rule-breaker from way back!)

Several weeks later, I had an assignment from *EEO Bimonthly* magazine – for $500! I almost cried. After that, I sold a similar article to an online magazine called *Edge*. The editor was so pleased with my work that he passed my name along to the magazine's sister publications. From that I ended up with supremely unglamorous – yet dollar-producing – assignments from *AKFCF Quarterly*, the magazine for KFC franchisees, and *QSR Success*, a magazine for the quick service restaurant industry (what you and I call "fast food joints").

Things took off from there, and soon I was writing part-time from the apartment I shared with my husband while working an office job three days per week.

When my husband transferred to a college near Boston in mid-1997, I decided to make the jump to full-time freelancing. We saved up enough money to squeak by for three months, with the understanding that if I didn't turn a profit by the end of that time, I would have to hit the want ads for a full-time position.

But I *did* turn a profit, and by working hard for trade magazines and smaller newsstand pubs, as well as for copywriting clients, I earned enough to support my husband and myself while he finished his degree.

Two years later, I was still loving the freelance lifestyle, but was frustrated that I hadn't been able to break into any of the larger newsstand magazines. Dozens of queries boomeranged with form rejections. But perseverance paid off, and one day I received a call from an editor at *Woman's Day* saying that she liked my idea – how to save money on big-ticket items like appliances and furniture – but that she preferred to see longer, better-researched queries. And here I had been following the one-page query rule like a good little writer! So I started writing two- and three-page queries, and that fall I landed lucrative assignments from *Woman's Day*, *Redbook*, and *Family Circle*. I had made it!

Feeling that I deserved a reward, I finally chucked the wood-look computer desk and ancient Mac I had been working on and sprang for nice new furniture and a blue iMac. I was ecstatic!

When my husband graduated from college, he decided to go freelance with me. Since I was trying to move up in the writing world, when my trade editors called with assignments, I told them that I could no longer work for 20 cents per word, but that my husband would be happy to give it a go. The hand-off worked, and Eric and I now write for many of the same magazines. At the same time, I dropped much of the boring copywriting work I had been doing to concentrate on magazines.

The freelancing life has been good to us. In 2000 we bought our first house, and since we started landing better-paying assignments, we've been able to cut our work schedule down to under 20 hours per week and still pay the bills. We have health insurance, we have retirement accounts, and we go on vacation every year. We also have time for hobbies, like reading and karate, and volunteer work.

I achieved this success only by breaking the rules of freelancing that writing magazines and books had tried to impose on me — rules that sound good to a beginner or novice but that in practice only served to trip me up. After years spent separating the phony from the bologna, I've learned that each writer needs to create his or her own rules.

Why we got together and wrote this book

Here's the story: In August 2000, Linda was lunching at a Thai restaurant in Boston with Ken Gordon, who at the time was her editor at *1099*, a magazine for freelancers. The conversation was all about writing, as it often is when writers gather, and Linda insisted that the one-page query letter rule was stupid; in fact, she said, she had better luck selling articles with three-page queries. "I should write an article on writing rules that should be broken," she huffed.

Introduction

"Forget the article," Ken said. "That would make a great book."

The proverbial light bulb went off in her head. A book!

Linda roped Diana into the project. When Linda told her about the concept, Diana immediately "got it." Although Diana had pored over books on freelance writing and listened to advice from more experienced journalists, she'd discovered along the way that she had more success when she followed her instincts or did the opposite of what everyone else was doing. Linda pulled a proposal together, and she and Diana wrote up three sample chapters.

Over the course of a year, Linda sent the proposal to 15 publishers. Each time, her self-addressed envelope came back fat with rejection – if it came back at all.

She also looked into teaming up with a well-known author who had a franchise of business books. Here's the deal he offered: Diana and Linda would do all the writing, editing, and promotion. The famous author's name would be listed first on the cover. And the famous author would pocket 50 percent of the royalties. Diana and Linda's counteroffer: Get bent.

Fast forward to September 2002 – more than two years after Linda had written the proposal. Out of nowhere, she received an e-mail from an editor she had written for at a printing industry trade magazine in the late 1990s when she was starting out.

"I now run a publishing company that publishes books for writers," he wrote. "Do you have any ideas for me?"

Did Linda have any ideas?! After wiping the tea from her monitor, she replied, "Why, yes, I just so happen to have a full-fledged proposal for a book about freelance writing languishing on my hard drive." After calling Diana to tell her the news, Linda put together the proposal and sample chapters and e-mailed them to the publisher.

Within a week we had a deal. The three of us hashed out the details of the contract, and it was settled. We were going to write a book!

And now you're holding that book in your hands. We hope that the advice you read here will get you started as a freelance writer or, if you're already freelancing, boost your success to the next level.

We're hardly veterans of the freelance life … between us, we have a mere 10 years of experience. So where do we get off writing a book about freelancing? Well, it's simple. We learned that the only rule is that there are no rules when it comes to success, and we didn't have to struggle for twenty years to figure that out. For every time we've read or heard that "your query letter should be no longer than one page," we've met two or three successful writers who sell regularly to top magazines with three- and four-page letters. (And we have, too.) We've used simultaneous submissions, ditched the SASE, called editors, sent queries via e-mail, and even queried magazines we had never read, and we know scores of other writers who have had success doing the same.

You'll see as you flip through each chapter of our book that each subhead is a "rule." We included rules that we've read in books and magazines, or that we've heard on the street (and online) from our peers. We also talked to a lot of writers who generously shared their rules – and rule-breaking experiences – with us. Many of these rules are serviceable, but need a tune-up. Other rules are simply outdated. For example, editors drum into our heads to read back issues of their magazines. But with the magazine industry in such flux, sometimes you're better off following other strategies to understand their editorial direction. You'll note that the rules sometimes even contradict one another – for example, "Public relations people are your friends," (p. 101) and "PR people are your enemies" (p. 103).

We advise you to skim the book and look for the rules that you've been following in your career, then read what we have to say about them. You may find that a small adjustment in your marketing strategy or writing process can make a big difference in your bottom line. If you're still drumming up the courage to make the jump into freelancing, the chapter "Starting Out" is for you. If you've been submitting one-page queries to one market at a time but you're experiencing so-so results, you definitely need to read our chapter on "Querying." And even if you're doing great,

Introduction

we still think you can boost your productivity and income by taking a closer look at the "rules" you've been working under.

The Renegade Writer

Chapter

One

Breaking in by Breaking Rules
Even New Freelancers Can Be Renegades

Misconceptions about getting started hold writers back. You may think that in order to be successful as a freelance writer, you need to go to journalism school, have an impressive database of editorial contacts, spend a truckload of money on supplies, and scrape your way through the bottom of the editorial barrel. Lies, lies, all lies! Read on to find out how you can get started now – even if your home office consists of the kitchen table and your most impressive "contact" is your pooch.

RULE: You need to attend journalism school or have a degree in English.

If that were so, magazines would certainly be a lot skinnier. Freelance writers come in all shapes, sizes, colors, and species – okay, maybe not species – and their backgrounds usually don't include degrees in English or journalism. Linda studied Slavic linguistics in graduate school. Her husband Eric, also a freelancer, has a degree in math. And while Diana minored in English as an undergraduate, her ten years in product marketing are what gave her the freelancing skills she needed to make it on the outside. Another freelancer we know, Kelly James-Enger, "escaped" from the law – that is, she trained as an attorney, but gave up litigation

25

in 1997 to become a successful health and fitness writer. We know other writers who've worked as nurses, teachers, and non-profit administrators prior to freelancing.

While having a degree in English or journalism can't hurt, it isn't a requirement, so don't go running off to the library to research financial aid schemes. You probably already have an educational or career background that puts you in a better position than some other freelancer who has only a fancy-schmancy degree in English lit. You're a CPA? Great! You'll have a leg up when pitching a story to *Cosmopolitan* on how smart gals can save for a rainy day. (Not to mention you'll be way ahead of other freelancers come April 15.) You practice medicine? There's a real need for writers with strong medical backgrounds to write health articles. A stay-at-home mom or dad with three children? Boy, what parenting magazine editors would give to pick your brain for a day. You probably carry enough raw material in there to pay for advanced degrees for all of your kids!

Do keep in mind, however, that the successful writers we know have a solid grasp of spelling, grammar, and the mind-boggling complexities of our language. Nothing – and we mean nothing – annoys editors more than getting a query letter filled with sorry spelling, ghastly grammar, and pitiful punctuation. We guarantee that if you commit these blunders, you won't have to worry about writing the article. If you suspect your writing is a prime candidate for the recycling bin, find someone who will be your informal editor before you send stuff out. *Pay* this saintly person if you have to, in cash or chocolate. Notice which mistakes you make over and over again, and learn how to fix them yourself. Keep a few grammar books and a dictionary near your computer, and when in doubt, look it up!

RULE: You need "connections."

Nope, this one just isn't true. Linda is proof positive of that. When she started freelancing in 1997, she didn't even know the

Chapter 1 - Breaking in by Breaking Rules

janitor at any of the magazines she was querying, never mind editors. All of the wonderful "connections" she has today came from good, hard work. Diana happened to know the editor who assigned her first article assignment at *Connecticut Magazine*, but after that, she targeted and broke into magazines with cold pitches.

We're not going to lie and tell you that connections won't help you; they will. Your proposal may get priority, or you may even get an assignment thrown your way. But what's more valuable to you and to any editor – whether she's someone you played bridge with in college or a stranger – are your timely ideas and professional attitude. They will take you further than the so-called "connections" lesser writers gnash their teeth over.

If you're still not convinced, don't worry: The connections you desire are simple to make. So simple, in fact, that we scratch our heads whenever we hear some poor mortal railing about another writer's success due to his "connections." Here's the deal. Say you e-mail several queries over a period of several months to a magazine. One day, instead of sending you yet another form rejection, the editor finally writes back and says, "Sorry, that last query didn't work for us. Feel free to send me more ideas though." Bingo – you've got yourself a connection. The next time you query her, you can write, "Thanks for inviting me to send you more ideas…."

But many writers don't consider that sort of interaction a connection, and they completely blow it off. They feel that a connection is someone who presents a 5,000-word assignment to them on a silver platter. If you are a good writer with lots of salable ideas, we assure you – you will soon have more editorial connections than you'll know how to handle.

Here are other ways smart writers develop connections:

■ **They keep in contact with editors who change jobs.** Diana, for example, worked with a terrific editor at *Psychology Today*. When the editor changed jobs and went to *Parenting*, Diana suddenly had an "in" at a magazine she'd been trying to crack for a year.

■ **They send introductory e-mails.** It's easy for an editor to ignore the pile of submissions growing on her desk, but it's also easy for most editors to respond to a friendly e-mail. This won't always work, but why not give it a try? We've had the best success with this strategy when approaching editors at trade magazines (magazines that target a specific industry).

■ **They meet with editors.** If you really want to make a personal connection, next time you're in New York (or near a publication's office elsewhere), ask an editor out for coffee. Even if they know you only from rejecting your pitches, many editors will respond favorably to such a request. Often, when they see that you're a witty, charming, intelligent coffee companion, they'll be even more receptive to your proposals.

■ **They ask editors for introductions.** There's nothing wrong with approaching an editor at Magazine A with whom you have good rapport and asking if she knows an editor at Magazine B who would be receptive to a proposal. If she does give you a name, consider this an awesome connection – you can start your introductory e-mail with, "My editor at Magazine A gave me your name…." In addition, if the magazine you're writing for has sister publications, you can ask your editor to introduce you to the editors at these other titles. When Linda mentioned to her editor at *Men's Fitness* that she had an idea for the magazine's sister publication, *Muscle & Fitness Hers*, her editor actually walked over to this magazine's editorial offices and passed her name on to the editors there. Soon, Linda had an assignment to write about alternative therapies for *Muscle & Fitness Hers*.

■ **They socialize with other writers.** It's classic "you scratch my back and I'll scratch yours." Linda and Diana, along with several other writers in their circle, regularly trade leads, contact names, and other valuable information.

RULE: You have to live in New York City to succeed.

Of all the successful freelance writers we know, only a handful live even close to the editor nexus known as Manhattan. Linda and Diana live outside of Boston, and we know writers who live in Kentucky, California, North Carolina, and even Greece, Australia, and England. In fact, the farther away you live from your editors, the more valuable you can be to them, because you can deliver stories and a perspective they won't find on Madison Avenue.

What's more, not every magazine has a New York-based editorial staff. *Shape*, for example, is based in Los Angeles, *Southern Living* and *Coastal Living* are in Alabama, and *The Atlantic Monthly*'s hallowed offices are in Boston. Location may be all-important in real estate, but you're selling ideas, not land — and ideas can be tracked down anywhere.

RULE: Starting a freelance career is expensive.

Let's see, you need letterhead, envelopes, business cards, a computer — make that a desktop computer *and* a laptop, because you'll be jetting all over the world, interviewing celebrities and business tycoons — a high-speed Internet connection, a....

Stop it already! Really, if you needed all this stuff, you'd have to slave at your day job nigh unto Doomsday to pay for it. Sure, it's nice to have, but when you're starting out, you need only the basics, especially if you're making a leap-of-faith jump into freelancing. If you are one of these brave souls, any extra money jingling in your pockets should be going toward life's little essentials like food, heat, shelter, and cat litter.

Even if you're lucky enough to have a partner or spouse who's footing your freelance apprenticeship, there's no need to go wild at Staples and Kinko's. We kid you not: Editors want nothing more than your good ideas presented professionally, so ditch the fancy letterhead and four-color business cards with your happy freelancing face smiling out of them. You can get by with good-quality white paper (bond is nice, but laser print will do), plain white envelopes, and access to a computer and printer. If you can afford a computer and printer, that's great – buy the best your wallet will bear. If you're strapped for cash, we suggest that you invest in this equipment as soon as your cash flow improves. You don't even need the most recent edition of that ol' freelancing bible, *Writer's Market*, because most every public library has a copy.

Diana used the proceeds from her first-ever magazine sale to purchase a 486 desktop PC (the best at the time), a Hewlett-Packard inkjet printer, and Microsoft Word. In case you're wondering, no, the amount she was paid didn't cover the cost of all these goodies, but she was still working at her marketing job at the time. She has since upgraded her PC – twice – and now works on an iMac. For letterhead, she set up a template in Word with her name, address, phone number and e-mail address above a solid line break. As for business cards, she had 500 black and white ones professionally printed (cost: $30) when she began meeting with editors. Her first office? A Queen Anne-style desk set up in the corner of her 12' x 12' single-gal bedroom.

Honestly, the start-up costs for a writing career can be quite modest. What can be expensive, however, is a wage-slave lifestyle footed by a freelance income. Say you've started getting assignments from editors while working a full-time job, and you decide to quit to write full-time. Your paychecks from a company usually come fairly regularly: some companies pay on the 15th and the 30th of the month, others pay every other Friday. Magazines don't work this way, unless you're on staff. Diana's first magazine article for *Connecticut Magazine* was assigned in the spring, but the deadline for copy wasn't until September. The editors then took another month to edit and approve her article, and then Diana had to wait an additional 30 days for payment, as specified in the contract. Her check finally arrived in time for the first snows of December. You do the math: a lot of rent payments and utility bills came due between the assignment and its check.

The bottom line: Save the money you think you need to spend

on fancy letterhead and business cards, stick it in a bank account, and learn how to live on less. Books and magazine articles generally advise entrepreneurs to stockpile enough cash to finance three to six months of living expenses, and we recommend leaning towards the half-year figure – despite Linda's speedy success – because nothing brings on a case of writer's block faster than the sound of your last dollars being sucked out of your checking account. Desperation rarely begets inspiration.

RULE: You have to build a library of writer's guidelines.

Linda has a whole box full of guidelines she's never looked at; reading the magazine, looking up the publication in *Writer's Market,* and maybe calling to verify the editor's name gives her all the information she needs. Not only that, but a full 30 percent of the magazines contacted about guidelines never even responded. If the magazines don't care enough to send guidelines, then obviously the guidelines aren't too important.

Diana also rarely sends for guidelines anymore. When she started freelancing in 1999, she compiled a stack of them in a three-ring binder that she has since misplaced – and not once has she gone looking for it. The game of musical chairs at most magazines makes guidelines pretty useless in her opinion: New editors like to shake things up and change direction faster than they can send new guidelines out. What she finds more useful is sitting at a bookstore café with the latest issue of a magazine she wants to write for and pretending she's an editor in an assigning mood. What kind of stories does the magazine seem to favor – first-person viewpoint, lots of reporting, or heavy on expert quotes? She can also tell a lot by looking at the masthead. Are freelancers writing the majority of articles? Or are staffers? Often Diana will get a dozen good ideas to pitch from that half-hour of fantasy play. If she's interested in writing for one of the magazine's departments, she simply calls the editorial office when she gets home and asks who assigns for that section.

If you still insist on getting guidelines, save a stamp and check out them out online (see Appendix 2, p. 187).

RULE: Don't ever write for free/cheap.

Should you make a habit of writing for free? No. Are there times when publishers exploit beginning writers by asking them to write for free? Yes, indeed. However, sometimes you may want to offer your services for free or cheap because you will get something out of the deal, even if that something doesn't pay the bills.

Here's an example: Diana recently pitched an idea to a trade magazine. The editor called to assign the piece, and when he offered $300 for 1,200 words, she almost laughed. Before she could seal the fate of the deal with a guffaw, she realized that this assignment would generate excellent publicity for the book you're holding in your hands, so she bit back her laughter and took the assignment.

Doing volunteer writing can give you clips while boosting your morale. A couple of years ago, feeling that she had to do something to remove the stain on her soul, Linda offered her writing services to the Massachusetts Society for the Prevention of Cruelty to Animals and provided articles for their newsletter gratis (until they hired an in-house writer to take over the job). Not only did the experience give Linda pet-related clips, but she soon noticed that paying work was flowing in faster than ever. Give, and good things will come to you.

If you do decide to write for free or cheap, we urge you to think hard about why you're doing it. If an editor with a new online magazine is urging you to write for free because you'll get "good exposure" or he says he can't afford to pay writers, you're probably being taken for a schnook. Move on. You can find better exposure in paying markets. But if you'll gain from the deal yourself or if the cause is something you believe in — animal welfare, human rights, or your kid's nursery school — go for it. Hey,

Diana once wrote book reviews for a website because she got free mystery and romance novels out of the deal.

RULE: Start at the bottom.

This self-imposed roadblock is one we read about or hear all the time ... that if you are a new writer, you should start out in the Little Leagues before angling for the Majors.

Plenty of writers began at the top. Kelly James-Enger is one of them; her first article assignment was from *Glamour*! And Diana's first assignment was from *Connecticut Magazine* – not exactly a brand-name magazine, but in her home state it's a magazine her friends and family read.

It probably sounds reasonable (and less scary) to approach a smaller, less visible publication if you're still wet behind the ears. You may believe that a rejection from *The Podunk Times* smarts less than one from *The New York Times*. Or you may have heard that smaller publications are eager to work with writers who don't have as many (or any) writing credits. Certainly we've heard from other writers, books, and magazines that these publications are far more receptive to writers than the ones you'll find lining the shelves at Borders or Barnes & Noble.

Diana strongly believes that if you're a new freelancer but have confidence in your skills and great, salable ideas, you can skip the weenie pubs and head for the top of the heap. When she started writing full time, she spent too much time querying smaller publications. She figured it would be easier to get work from the smaller publications, but she found that they had smaller staffs and budgets, so they were very unresponsive, or they'd offer her something like $25 for 1,000 words. Ugh. Sorry, but she likes to pay her bills.

Once, Diana had a terrific idea that she pitched to some local newspapers, which never responded. Then she realized that the story was perfect for *The New York Times*. She fired off a query to the editor who handled the section she wanted to write for, and within an hour, he wrote back, advising her to contact another staff editor about the idea. She did, and the next morning, the second editor wrote back, declining the idea (since they'd done something similar a few months back), but inviting her to send more ideas. This was enough for Diana to realize that she'd rather get a friendly, polite rejection from *The New York Times* than be ignored by the 2-cents-per-word local rags stacked for free in her neighborhood grocery store.

Now, before you come after us with a tire iron for insulting small magazines, we do know that plenty of low-paying, local publications employ appreciative, bright editors who treat your copy with the respect it's due. We even write for a few of these publications because their PITA (Pain In The Ass) rating is low. But don't let some stupid rule about "paying your dues" prevent you from querying *The Wall Street Journal* or *Smithsonian* or any other top-name publication. You shouldn't put all your eggs in one basket by querying only the big guys, of course, but don't be afraid to take a crack at them – even if you're a beginner. If you're already a good writer, go for it – you have nothing to lose and everything to gain. And if the biggies don't bite, you always have the smaller guys as a backup.

RULE: Editors don't want to see newspaper clips.

Often, you'll hear magazine pros tell newbie writers that if they want to impress an editor at a glossy magazine, they shouldn't send newspaper clips because newspapers are the bastard children of the publishing world.

Funny, but many writers we know started out writing for newspapers. While Diana held a full-time technical writing job, she did countless feature stories for a chain of newspapers in Boston on everything from honeymoon planning to growing lilacs. And guess what? The editor she approached at *Walking* liked the newspaper clips she showed him. Linda also wrote for a newspaper when she was starting out. Besides that, we know a few writers who were full-time newspaper journalists before they wrote for magazines, and they certainly used their newspaper clips when they started out.

It's not the medium, it's the message. And the message is this: Editors like good writing. If you've written truly wonderful pieces, and they happen to have appeared in your local newspaper, few editors are going to hold your package at arm's length as if it smells like doody. (Needless to say, if you boast clips from *The New York Times*, *The Christian Science Monitor*, or *The Wall Street Journal*, few editors will scoff at your work.)

RULE: If you write "shorts" for a magazine, you'll never break in to the "feature well."

Many writers have very strong opinions about writing "shorts," those 200- to 500-word articles found mostly at the front of a magazine. Some freelancers won't touch them, claiming they're too much work for not enough pay, or that once you're pegged as a "shorts writer" by a magazine, you'll find it harder to convince that magazine's editors that you can handle more complicated stories. Other freelancers claim that shorts writing is an excellent way to crack a target publication, and that once you've bonded with your assigning editor, she'll be more receptive to pitches for longer stories. Diana found the whole debate of "shorts" versus "no shorts" so fascinating that she wrote an article about it for *The Writer*!

Our take? It depends. We lean toward the pro-shorts side if you're a new freelancer or if you've had no luck interesting an editor in your longer story pitches. Also, certain magazines start new-to-them writers out on shorter pieces before giving them feature work. This happened to Diana when she approached *Contract Professional* magazine; they gave her a few brief department pieces at first, but when she proved herself a dependable, straightforward writer, the editor started assigning her 1,500- to 2,500-word features and cover stories.

We think that many magazines are more receptive to new writers who are willing to write shorts rather than those who hold out for bigger assignments. If a new writer screws up on a 200-word short, the resulting hole in the magazine isn't that big, so an editor is more apt to take that risk. If the writer screws up on a 2,000-word piece, the editor suddenly has four pages to fill — and your name is mud. Also, most magazines have more shorts than features, which means more opportunities for freelancers (unless, of course, the shorts are staff-written).

Now, the flip side. Yes, you could be pegged as a shorts writer by your editor — that's the chance you take if you follow this strategy. However, you can protect yourself with these steps:

■ **Don't keep pitching short stuff.** That seems self-evident, you sow what you reap. If you continually query 200-word news items, you're simply encouraging your editor to think of you as "the hot writer in shorts."

■ **As you write longer stories for other publications (especially competing pubs), send the clips to your editor with a friendly note.** No one likes to be poached from, and we wager that your editor will soon call with a bigger assignment.

■ **If, despite all this, you sense that you're not going anywhere with your assigning editor, cut bait and move on.** If she calls you with a short, fast assignment, decline it and tell her that you've decided to concentrate on longer features. This may be the last time you hear from her, but on the other hand, it could be the kick in the jumpseat that she needs. Although Kelly James-Enger writes the occasional short, she recently decided to tell her editors, "I really appreciate you thinking of me, but I've decided to cut back on short pieces for the time being. I find they take nearly as much time to write as longer features and I've got more work than I can handle right now. I am interested in doing longer pieces for you, but I'll have to pass on the shorts." Doing this didn't guarantee feature work — in fact, she didn't hear from some of the editors again. "But not doing them freed me up to pitch, research, and write features which pay much better, so it was worth it in the end," she says.

If you're a more experienced freelancer, then we suggest skipping the "shorts-to-feature" route. There are better ways for you to get noticed. But don't rule out shorts completely. If you've been pitching features to a target magazine with no luck, and then one day an editor calls with a quick 300-word assignment, it could be time to bite the bullet. For example, Linda's husband Eric submitted a query to *Woman's Day* for a full article on ways to honor your country. The editor asked Eric to write the idea as a short sidebar that could be appended to an article they were publishing about volunteering. Eric said yes, and has since landed longer assignments from this magazine.

Also, if you've written longer features for a publication, and then they ask you to do a short, why not take the assignment? If you're a fast writer, they're usually a couple of hours of work, and if you can get a good per-word rate, the hourly rate can be excellent. For example, 300 words at $1 per word = $300. $300 divided by approximately two hours of research and writing time = $150 per hour. Not too shabby!

Chapter

Two

Cranking Up the Idea Factory
Bold Thinking Leads To Countless Ideas

Coming up with salable ideas is all about lying, cheating, and stealing: Lying by writing about topics you know nothing about, cheating by playing games instead of working, and stealing by nabbing topics from government reports, books, and even other articles. Wondering how a life of crime can turn you into an idea-generating writing machine? Keep reading and we'll tell you.

RULE: Don't steal ideas.

News Flash: Ideas can't be copyrighted, so ideas can't be stolen. Feel free to take ideas that you find and sell them to magazines yourself. Here's a list of buried treasure waiting to be pilfered:

■ **Newsletters**. Linda gets a monthly newsletter from a food safety organization, and one article that caught her eye defined common food additives, such as guar gum, lactic acid, and Yellow #5 (yum). Linda pitched that same idea to *Oxygen* magazine – and sold it.

■ **Government reports**. If the U.S. government is good at one thing, it's churning out information, all of which can be mined for article ideas. For example, the web site of the U.S. Department of Agriculture has discussed the new national standards for organic foods and the conclusion of the U.S.-Chile Free Trade Agreement. What great ideas for articles! And believe it or not, materials published by the government are copyright-free, so feel free to steal, loot, pillage and plunder.

■ **Press releases.** Hey, that's what the releases are there for – to get press. Say you like to write about science – you can get scientific press releases from Eurekalert.org. You can also ask to be put on the press lists of such organizations as NASA and NOAA (the National Oceanic & Atmospheric Administration).

■ **Trade magazines.** Articles in trade magazines can often be turned into features for a much broader audience. For example, a writer for *Funworld*, which is read by amusement industry professionals, used his bank of industry expertise to sell an article about roller coasters to a large national magazine. Even if you're not an expert in the fields of microbiology, sheep raising, or call centers, you can often glean ideas from mags devoted to such fields.

■ **Regional magazines and newspapers.** A regional idea may have more far-reaching appeal. Many national magazines want stories about exceptional people, successful businesses, and so on, and regional pubs are where these subjects will first appear. Susan Orlean's "The Orchid Thief," composed of essays she first wrote for *The New Yorker*, sprang from articles she'd read in Florida newspapers that caught her eye that she then researched and expanded upon.

■ **Consumer magazines.** Okay, you wouldn't want to take an article about forgotten bands of the 1960s from *Rolling Stone* and query the idea to its competitor, *Spin*. But why not query a similar idea to *My Generation*, the magazine for baby boomers? Or how about an article on forgotten films of the 1960s for *Premiere*?

Chapter 2 - Crank up the Idea Factory

■ **Books**. Magazine editors like topics that are made timely by the publication of a new book. So when Linda saw the new book "Semi-homemade Cooking" by Sandra Lee, she pitched a story about how to make store-bought foods look homemade. The bonus to this is that she had a ready-made source – the book's author. Diana also regularly flips through the psychology and self-help books at bookstores to come up with ideas for relationship articles.

■ **Your own articles.** Once you've done the work of coming up with, selling, researching, and writing an idea, you should get as much mileage out of it as possible. For example, Linda once wrote an article for *Redbook* called "The Better Orgasm Diet," about foods that boost the libido. She then reslanted the idea for men, queried it, and landed an assignment from *Men's Fitness* called "Vanity Fare," about foods that improve your hair, breath, and physique to make you more desirable to women. Linda also wrote about how to write a press release for *1099* magazine, and then later sold the same idea to HomeOfficeJournal.com.

But how can you steal ideas from others without feeling a twinge of guilt – or at least fearing that an editor will realize you pilfered your topic? Here are questions to ask to help you make any idea your own:

■ **How could this writer have done better?** Say you see an article about online investing that you think is a little weak. The writer didn't use many experts and instead relied on anecdotes from successful amateur investors. Well, maybe you can pitch a story on "Experts' Secrets for Winning in Online Investing."

■ **What is the opposite of this topic?** You read an article in a business magazine about unique advertising techniques that work. Why not pitch a story about advertising methods that *don't* work, or famous ad flops? As another example, Linda once wrote an article about selling to women's magazines for *Writer's Digest* mag-

41

azine. A few months later, she pitched a story about writing for *men's* magazines to *The Writer*. Within a week, she had an assignment.

■ **Who else would be interested in this idea?** Eric saw a small piece in *Reader's Digest* about the National Wife-Carrying Championships taking place the following month in Bethel, Maine. Who else would be interested in this news? Game magazines, of course! Eric sold a short piece about the competition to *GAMES*, and got a fun, tax-deductible trip to Maine to boot.

■ **How can I make this idea regional?** An article in a cooking magazine about Ethiopian cuisine can be translated into an article about Ethiopian restaurants in Rhode Island for a local magazine.

■ **How can I make this regional idea national?** When Diana picked up her college's alumnae magazine a couple of years ago and read about an etiquette seminar the college sponsored during winter break, she thought the etiquette consultant who ran the seminar would be perfect for a career profile at *1099* – and *1099* thought so, too.

■ **How can I make this idea narrower?** If you run across an article in a health magazine about the popularity of martial arts, you can query an article about how to get started in tae kwan do or krav maga.

■ **How can I make this idea broader?** Linda once wrote an article about how to peel a banana – admittedly, a very narrow topic. A smart writer would have stolen that idea and turned it into an article about tips for preparing and cooking fruit.

Chapter 2 - Crank up the Idea Factory

RULE: Always keep a pen and paper on your nightstand to capture great ideas you have at night.

You jolt awake at 3 a.m. with a brilliant idea. You grab for the pen and paper you keep by your bed, scribble down your idea, then drift back to la-la land.

In the morning, you wake up and eagerly grab for your paper. "Unicyclists," it says. "Underwear for cats and dogs."

Not everyone comes up with brilliant ideas in bed, although the way the writing books and magazines have it, if you don't have a pen and paper on your nightstand, you're throwing away money in your sleep. We've spoken to many writers who say their best ideas come to them while they're driving, shopping, talking to a neighbor, or taking a shower. So don't panic if your nocturnal brain emissions aren't all that brilliant. We're sure you get your brain spurts in other places as well.

Linda carries a small notebook and pen with her everywhere. When she comes up with a new idea or sees a new magazine on the stands that she'd like to pitch a story to, she scribbles it down in her notebook.

Diana keeps a small tape recorder in her car so she can dictate her ideas without having to juggle a pen and paper. You can also find notebooks that attach to the dashboard of the car so you can write one-handed.

Like many other writers, Diana gets her best ideas in the shower. So she keeps a tube of cheap lipstick handy, and whenever a great idea lathers up, she jots it down on the shower stall wall. When she's all dressed and ready to head downstairs, she transfers her shower jottings into a notebook and scrubs off the lipstick with a shower brush. (If you try this, test the lipstick-and-wall combo first. Do you really want "sex in fun places" permanently visible in your shower stall?)

RULE: Predict what the editor will assign by reading past issues of the publication.

It helps to look to the past, but even better is to look to the future – the magazine's editorial calendar. The editorial calendar is a list of the features and themes a magazine plans to publish in the upcoming year, and is created by the advertising department to convince potential advertisers to buy ad space.

Getting the editorial calendar may be tricky, but it can be worth the effort. Since the calendar lists the themes for each issue, you can come up with ideas that fit into the themes and pitch them to the editor. When Eric got the editorial calendar for *Playthings* magazine, for example, he saw that one issue would be devoted to board games and puzzles. Bingo! He queried the editor on an article about merchandising board games – something he happened to have a lot of experience in.

To get your hot little hands on an editorial calendar, your first stop is the magazine's website, which sometimes has the calendar posted in the advertisers' section and sometimes with the writer's guidelines. If you can find the editorial calendar online, you're in, as they say, like Flynn.

If that doesn't work, try calling the magazine's advertising department – the number is usually listed in the magazine's masthead. Sometimes the person who answers the phone will send you a calendar no questions asked. But other times, they screen their requests to make sure that the editorial calendar goes out only to potential advertisers and not to, say, competitors or writers looking to break in to the magazine. In fact, you might want to e-mail or write to the advertising department instead of calling, since they'll be less likely to ask questions.

RULE: Write what you know.

If Linda had to write only about topics she's had personal experience in, the possibilities would be limited to writing, Slavic

Chapter 2 - Crank up the Idea Factory

linguistics, karate and how to peel a banana. But instead, she's taken the idea "Write what you don't know" to heart, and has published articles about artificial intelligence, game theory, what astronauts eat on the space shuttle, migrant health care, trolley parks, customer relationship management, natural health care for pets, and much more.

Linda became a jack-of-all trades early on. In 1997 and 1998, she wrote articles for trade magazines like *QSR* (Quick Service Restaurant) *Success*, *Mini Storage Messenger*, *Pastry Art & Design*, and *Party & Paper Retailer*. She would contact trade magazines with an introduction letter (see #TK: "You have to query to get an assignment"), and they would call her with assignments on a variety of topics. They didn't care that Linda had no experience in these industries because with a pay rate of 30 cents per word or less, these magazines couldn't afford to be picky – they simply needed a good writer, cheap.

Knowing that she could write about, say, how to create a jicama display or how mini-storage facility owners can hire the best employees gave Linda the confidence to query magazines on other subjects that she didn't know much about. She soon sold an article about careers in game theory to *American Careers* and a piece about extended-wear contact lenses to *Edge*.

Eventually, Linda built up multiple niches that she could write about with ease: business, science, health, nutrition, careers, pets, women's interest, and kids' interest.

When it comes to selling articles that are out of your range of experience, success builds on itself. If you start out with the attitude that you can research and write about anything, you will keep getting assignments on topics that are out of your ken. The wider variety of assignments you complete, the more confident editors will be in assigning you stories on topics in which you have no previous experience.

So don't feel that you can write only about your own hobbies and personal experiences. Take a chance and branch out by researching and writing queries that are a stretch for you.

RULE: You need to generate lots of ideas.

New ideas are good, but old ideas can be better. Instead of racking your brain to come up with the Next Big Idea, why not recycle the ideas you've already written about?

In 1998, Linda wrote an article for *Walking* called "The Bitter Truth," about people who are genetically predisposed to hate vegetables. Because she sold only First North American Serial Rights to the magazine, Linda was free to sell the article elsewhere. So she sent it to *Vibrant Life*, which paid her about $150 for the article – not too bad for two minutes' work. She then took the information from the article, condensed it into a much shorter piece, and sold it to *FitnessLink*. A couple of years later, Linda rewrote the idea for *Men's Fitness*.

Linda also sold an article about how to maintain a positive online image to *Business Start-Ups*, and then resold the idea to *Minority Engineer*, CareerMag.com, and *Succeed*. She earned several hundred dollars by making minor changes to the article for each market.

Kelly James-Enger is the guru of reprints; in fact, she wrote a chapter about reprints for "Trade Secrets: A Professional Guide to the Business of Nonfiction Freelance Writing," published by the American Society of Journalists and Authors (ASJA). In 2000 she was writing for national magazines but realized there were other markets (primarily smaller mags or regional pubs) that might be interested in her articles, especially the evergreen topics (those topics that magazines turn to again and again). "These markets don't pay as much as national mags, but it's essentially 'free' money," she says.

James-Enger had a slew of evergreen bridal stories on subjects like getting along with your in-laws, talking about money, and dealing with wedding planning stress, so she searched for regional bridal markets using books like Standard Rate & Data Services' media guides (see Appendix 3, p. 188). She called the mags, asked if they'd be interested in reprints, and then sent packages with sample articles and a list of available story ideas. Then she followed up on them. Using this method, James-Enger has sold to about a half-dozen bridal markets throughout the country. Some buy only one or two articles, but others have bought many pieces from her over several years.

James-Enger then started looking for possible health and fitness reprint markets. This was tougher, but she's found a couple of markets that buy her articles. She contacts them every three to four months to let them know what new stories she has available for reprint.

"I don't know how many articles I've reprinted – I'd guess about 25, but several of those have sold more than once," James-Enger says. "My biggest hits have been the bridal ones – a couple of those have sold three or four times, and I continue sending them out when I find new regional markets. I'll also occasionally offer what I call 'tweaks' where I revise the original story for the new market – for example, editing a diet story that originally ran in a woman's magazine so it's appropriate for a bridal mag. I still consider it a reprint, though, and market it accordingly." In the past two years James-Enger has made about $5,000 from reprinted work.

Here's how you can duplicate James-Enger's success: When you're assigned an article that you think has the potential to sell to other magazines, do everything you can to get a contract that claims only First North American Serial Rights to the article. This means that the magazine has the right to be the first magazine to run your article; after that, the rights to the article revert back to you. (See "The contract is set in stone," p. 83)

Once your article has been published in the first magazine, use *Writer's Market* to find markets that accept reprints. Linda likes to use the online version, WritersMarket.com (which costs about $30 per year), because you can search for magazines based on whether they accept reprints. If you use the print version, you'll have to read every magazine entry to find out which ones might buy your reprints.

Then, create a letter that will make editors drool with anticipation over the idea of reading your article. Here's the letter Linda used to sell reprints of "The Bitter Truth":

> Dear Ms. Publishme:
>
> Look through just about any magazine and you'll see an article advising its readers to turn to vegetables for anti-cancer compounds and disease-fighting fiber. These health benefits are great news for vegetable lovers. But where does that leave those of us who think veggies are vile?
>
> There are more of us than you think. In fact, new studies show there is an entire group of people – "supertasters," people who are very sensitive to bitterness – who are likely to scorn veggies.
>
> In "The Bitter Truth," I talked with taste researchers and nutritionists to tell veggie-hating readers how to satisfy their nutritional requirements through means other than vegetables and how to *really* disguise the vegetables in their meals so they can get the nutrients they need and worry less about their health.
>
> The first North American rights for "The Bitter Truth" were purchased by Walking magazine and the story appeared in the October 1998 issue. I'm offering reprint rights to the piece. Will you share this article with your readers?
>
> Best regards,
> Linda Formichelli

There's no need to include clips, since you're sending the entire article, but you can include a SASE if you have a burning desire to keep track of your rejections (see "Always include a self-addressed stamped envelope (SASE) with your query," p. 60).

Chapter 2 - Crank up the Idea Factory

RULE: Ideas are all around you.

We firmly believe that you can pull ideas out of every aspect of your life. So why are we refuting that here?

Well, it's true that ideas are everywhere – but sometimes it's tough to catch them as they whiz through your frontal lobes. If you're feeling like you couldn't grab a good idea if it walked up and kicked you in the shins, try these tactics:

■ **Play a game.** Diana, Linda, and Eric came up with a game to rev up the idea-generating process. One of them would throw out a word, and then they'd all try to think up ideas related to that word. "Green," Diana challenged at their last session. "An inside look at how money is made," Eric offered. "Tips from golf course owners on how to care for your lawn," Linda suggested. "How to deal with friends who are green with envy over your successes," said Diana. The word "tea" inspired such ideas as ten things to do with tea (such as antiquing linens or adding shine to dark hair), how to brew the perfect pot, and a look at teapots and the people who collect them.

■ **Read outside the box.** Another way to overcome writer's block is to check out magazines that you wouldn't normally read. Browsing through *Aeronautics Monthly* or *Modern Ferret* not only helps you find fresh ideas that you can reslant for other markets, but it also introduces you to a whole new world of writers and writing styles. And you can do this anytime you want, gratis, by going to your local bookstore café, gathering up armloads of magazines from sections you rarely peruse, and reading them over a cup of java.

■ **Get a kick in the pants.** Linda is a freelance writer. That means she gets up at 11, sits in front of a computer all day, and spends her spare time in bookstores and cafés with other writers who get up at 11 and sit in front of computers all day. The problem is, a humdrum life leads to humdrum ideas.

So one day, Linda surprised herself – and gave her ideas a shot of adrenaline – by signing up for karate classes. Soon she was spending several hours a week kicking, punching, and yelling, which is pretty much the opposite of researching, interviewing, and stringing nouns and verbs. What a wake-up call! She's met kindergarten teachers, sound system engineers, and people who work with gibbons at the zoo – all with fascinating stories to tell. She also ended up selling an article on the benefits of martial arts to *Oxygen* magazine.

For Linda, karate was the answer, but for other writers it may be bowling, in-line skating, the local softball league – anything that gets the heart pumping and the mind off of writing. Come to think of it, any class, from flower arranging to American history, can shake up a writer's life.

■ **Mine your life.** For Diana, the creative boot came from starting a family. When she and her husband learned they were expecting a baby, suddenly a whole new market opened up for her: parenting magazines! She pitched stories on new advances in prenatal testing and essays about strangers who were compelled to touch her enormous belly. Then when her son was born, she realized she not only got a great kid, but she got a little moneymaker, too (something she points out to her husband when he complains about how much it costs to raise a kid). She lugged her six-month-old to a child modeling agency to research a proposal on agency scams, and even the drool cascading over his lips became fodder for a *Parenting* magazine piece. Having a baby gave her entry into a whole new world – mother's groups, playgroups, doctor's offices, the highway at 3 a.m. when her son was teething – and gave her a motherlode of great story ideas.

We don't recommend you run out and get yourself or your mate in the family way for the sole purpose of spicing up your writing life, but think about recent major life changes. Are you getting married next year? Think bridal magazines. Did you just dump your girlfriend? What about a funny relationship piece for a men's magazine? Have you changed your diet and exercise habits and lost 50 pounds? Consider a reported essay on safe weight loss for a health and fitness magazine.

■ **Take off.** Sometimes you have to empty your mind of all the junk that's bouncing around in there to make room for new, fresh ideas to come in – and what better way than to take a break? Once, Linda was hit with a writer's block the size of Montana; all her ideas were stale, boring, lame. So she cleared a couple of days on her schedule, packed her bags, and headed up to New Hampshire for some R&R at a B&B. Soaking in a hot tub and drinking port in front of a roaring fire certainly helped her forget about writing for a little while – and when she got back to the office, the ideas started flowing again.

Diana finds it a little harder to take off for B&Bs, but she has other ways to take breaks. Friday night at her house is "Mom's Night Out." She leaves the little one with Dad, who's usually parked in front of "Star Trek: The Next Generation" for the evening, while she goes to a local bookstore to chill. After a long week of writing combined with childcare and housework, Diana is brain dead, but a few hours of drinking coffee, flipping through magazines, and pretending that there's not a dirty diaper waiting for her when she gets home revitalizes her.

Taking a break doesn't always require a lot of free time and cash. Even one day of reading on the couch instead of staring frustrated at a computer screen can bring on an infusion of creativity. Linda used to work through the weekends in a fit of Type-A pique, but she realized that she can face Mondays with much more creative energy if she gives herself the weekend to read, explore the town, and hang out with her friends.

Diana once took a week off from querying to clean and organize her office. With lots of empty surface space in front of her and all her files in order, Diana could focus better on idea generating.

RULE: Never share your ideas with other writers.

Did you ever have a great idea that you couldn't bear to write? Say you came up with an idea about how do-it-yourselfers should know when to call in a professional for help – when they don't have the correct tools for a job, for instance, or when a job is too complicated for non-professionals. You know this idea would sell to one of the many homeowners' magazines out there. It's a great idea!

But day after day, that idea grows moldier and moldier on your to-do list. Even though you're sure it will sell, you're too busy to bother … or maybe, as great as the idea is, it's not something you'd be interested in researching and writing. Why not pass the idea along to a friend who can cash in on it?

Linda once called Diana to whine that she had nothing good to pitch to her editors. (You see? Everyone goes through writing troughs, even an experienced freelancer like Linda!) Diana had hundreds of great ideas, but no time to get them circulating. She figured, "Why not share them with a friend?" So she whipped out her bulging idea file and passed a bunch of really good ones to Linda. Wow, did that change Linda's mood! She took a few of them, and right there on the phone, reslanted them to fit her target publications. The next day she called Diana back and informed her that one of the ideas had sold to *Men's Fitness* for $1,600! Later, she reslanted the idea, pitched it to *Family Circle*, and tallied another $2,500 for the effort.

One of Diana's other writing buddies said, "Man, you must have been pissed that you didn't pitch that story yourself." Actually, she was almost as thrilled as Linda was! The way Diana looks at it, there have been plenty of times Linda has bailed her out of a pit of despair or let Diana use her name with an editor at Magazine X. Diana knows there simply isn't enough time in the day to write every good story that crosses her path, so until she figures out a way to make 24 hours stretch even longer, it makes perfect sense to pass on what she can't use to someone who can.

We urge all of you to look around at your writing cohorts. Is there someone who could use a little of your help? If so, don't be stingy – offer to give them a few ideas, or brainstorm with them – and don't be surprised if you feel a little better about yourself in the process! Besides, the next time you hit an idea slump, the people you helped in the past may come to your rescue. (P.S. Linda, you owe me lunch.)

Chapter

Three

No-Fear Querying
Now Turn Those Ideas Into Assignments

No part of writing is as rife with misconceptions as querying. Would you believe that you can write two- or even three-page query letters, ditch the self-addressed stamped envelopes, query magazines you've never read, and even land assignments without querying at all? Well, believe it, because it's all true.

RULE: Buy six back issues of magazines before querying.

Here's a paradox: Editors expect writers to read the last six issues of their magazine before querying – but what magazine writer can afford back issues of every publication she's targeting? Of course, it doesn't hurt circulation numbers to have all us poor, hapless writers shelling out dollars down at the newsstand month after month.

If you really feel compelled to read six issues of your target magazine like all the other books say you should, spring for a year's subscription, since that will often be cheaper than six newsstand copies. Even cheaper is to check your bill inserts and membership reward programs for special deals. For example, American Express sometimes lets you use membership points to "buy" subscriptions to magazines. Diana has used her points to subscribe to *Glamour*, *Writer's Digest*, and *Town & Country*. (Be aware, however, that renewals may be automatically charged to your credit card. Keep good records!)

When Linda first started freelancing, she stuck a note in her neighbors' mailboxes asking them to drop their used magazines on her front porch instead of into the recycling bin. More than learning about her neighbors' tastes in reading materials, Linda learned about magazines she never knew existed. She also has a deal with her hairdresser to periodically cart away the piles of magazines that threaten to take over the shop.

These aren't the only ways to score reading material on a budget:

■ **Visit your town's recycling center.** Freelancer Sheilagh Casey's town has a trailer dedicated to recycled magazines and slick junk mail.

■ **Look for "magazine swaps."** Before relocating, Kelly James-Enger frequented a library that had a "magazine swap." "People could leave magazines they no longer wanted and take whatever ones caught their eye," she says. You can also start a swap with your other freelancing friends.

■ **Get up really early on Saturday mornings and haunt yard sales**. Writer Beth Lee Segal relies on tag and garage sales to buy back issues of magazines.

■ **Ask your friends, co-workers, and relatives for recent magazines.** When Diana was working full-time in an office, she asked co-workers to bring in old magazines from home. She asked specifically for the types of magazines she wanted to write for and received stacks of pubs in return.

■ **Go work out or get checked out**. Freelancer Iyna Bort Caruso has good luck browsing trade and consumer magazines at the gym. Or if you're due for teeth cleaning or a cholesterol check, ask your dentist or doctor if you can clean out their waiting rooms.

■ **Sign up for a free trial.** Magazines entice readers with offers of no-questions-asked free trial subscriptions, which writers like Don Hinkle take advantage of.

■ **Hop aboard planes, trains, and other vehicles.** Writer Arline Zatz swears by airport terminals. "If you go through the main Continental Airlines terminal building at Newark Airport, you'll find at least a dozen magazines with subjects unknown to many – and good outlets for various work," she says. "They're free for the taking."

■ **Browse the bookstore.** Diana makes weekly trips to her local Barnes & Noble and Borders to check out what's new on the racks.

RULE: Keep queries to one page.

For her first two years of freelancing, Linda sent one-page queries to top women's markets like a good little girl. Then, one day, an editor from *Woman's Day* called and said she preferred to see more research in queries. Within two months, two- and three-page queries landed Linda assignments with *Redbook*, *Woman's Day* and *Family Circle*. Moreover, Diana points out that her first freelance assignment resulted from a two-page, single-spaced query. She continues to ignore the one-page mandate and has happily made many sales despite her naughty behavior. Freelancer Roxanne Nelson recently sent a three-page query to *The Atlantic Monthly*, and received an encouraging response from the editor. And, as she points out, "With online queries, you can't really see the page breaks!"

Other editors agree that bigger is better. "Since ours is a

health magazine, I'd rather see a longer, better-researched query that gives me some indication the writer knows what he or she is talking about," says Denise Foley, deputy editor of *Prevention*. "Actually, most queries I get reflect a lack of depth and sophistication about health issues."

We're not saying that every query has to rival "War and Peace." If you've worked with the editor before, a quick outline of your idea may be all that she needs to give you the go-ahead. Diana, for example, has had success sending informal one-paragraph queries via e-mail. And as she was writing this chapter, Linda won a $600 assignment from *Writer's Digest* from a two-sentence pitch. Not a bad return from a query that took a minute to write!

Some magazines do prefer shorter pitches. When she was interviewing editors of men's magazines for an article in *The Writer*, Linda found that they liked queries to be as short as possible. "Women tend to be more chatty, so you can write longer queries for women's magazines," one editor said. "Men are more blunt and to the point."

So here's a tip: Tailor the length of your query to your topic and to the type of magazine you're pitching. If you need two or more pages to include all the research you think is relevant, go for it. Don't fret if your query spills onto a second or even a third page: it won't be a dealbreaker if your query rocks. On the other hand, if you have an idea for a men's mag that takes one short and snappy paragraph to explain, then write one paragraph – no more.

RULE: No simultaneous querying.

Let's get this straight. You mean that you're supposed to send your query to one magazine, wait up to 12 weeks (or longer) for a response – by which time your query is probably out of date – then send it on to the next magazine on your list? If magazine editors can't report back in a decent amount of time, then they'll have to accept that in order to buy groceries and pay the electric company, writers must send simultaneous submissions.

When Linda was starting out, she'd mail merge her queries with the contact information from up to 15 magazines on her database program. She'd examine the resulting letters on her monitor to make sure the merge went through and to personalize the letters as needed. For example, she might want to offer a 600-word article to certain magazines and a 1,500-word article to others, based on her research of the publications. She'd then set up an assembly line of letters, clips, envelopes, SASEs, and stamps, put together the packages, and drop them in the mail. Linda sold a good number of her queries this way.

Now, we're not advising you to write generic queries and send them out en masse; you absolutely should add customized details to your letters. You'll need to change the names of the departments you're pitching to, the word counts you're proposing, or anything else that's unique to the magazine. We suggest keeping a checklist at hand so that you don't overlook any of these important details.

Still afraid that the gods watching over Madison Avenue will smite you in your sleep if you send out simultaneous queries? Then try slanting the same idea for different types of publications. For example, Linda sent a query about "How Your Lifestyle Affects Your Dog" to *Dog Fancy*, then turned around and sent "How Your Lifestyle Affects Your Cat" to *Cat Fancy*. She could probably also reslant the query for magazines about horses, llamas, birds – whatever. If two magazines accept the query, you can take on both assignments, as long as you're careful not to hand in the same article to each one.

We recommend simultaneous querying when you don't have a personal connection with the magazines you're pitching. However, when you have a few editor contacts on your speed dial, you'll probably want to give the editors you've worked with an exclusive on your idea before mailing it out to the magazine industry at large. If Linda has a great idea for an article on saving money, she'll now send it to her editor at *Woman's Day* and wait for her response before sending it on to *Ladies' Home Journal*, *Good Housekeeping*, and so on. Why? First, out of loyalty to a magazine that has given her work in the past. Second, she'll probably get a faster response from *Woman's Day* since she's a known quantity to the editor.

So you've decided to turn to simultaneous queries to help get the checks rolling in. What if two magazines accept your query at once? Unlikely, but if it does happen, there are ways to deal. Dancing the happy dance is one of them. Accepting the assignment from the better magazine and suggesting a different topic twist to the second magazine is another. And offering first serial rights to one magazine and second serial rights to the other is a third way. See? We said there are ways to deal. (And may you always have such problems.)

RULE: Always include a self-addressed stamped envelope (SASE) with your query.

Most books, and many professional writers, insist that you include a SASE in your query. To not do so, according to these sages, is to proclaim your unprofessionalism, your boorishness, your amateurism, ad nauseam. But do you hear that grumbling? That's the sound of professional writers who have dutifully included SASEs with their queries and submissions only to have their envelopes seemingly disappear into the ether. Or, like Diana, they notice that the rejection letter comes to them in the magazine's own envelope.

"As a barely published beginner, I always include a SASE unless the magazine's guidelines advise not to," says freelance writer Karen Dove Barr. "I get a rejection slip back in my SASE about two-thirds of the time. The rest of the time I am sending my work and my unused stamp and good envelope into outer space." Linda may not be a beginner anymore, but her experience matches Barr's: A full 30 percent of her SASEs never return to her ink-stained hands. We suspect that unresponsive magazines are part of an underground stamp ring that peels the postage off writers' SASEs and sells them on the black market. Pretty tricky!

Chapter 3 - No-Fear Querying

Outside the fantasy world of underground stamp rings, SASEs (and the queries they're attached to) may go AWOL for any number of reasons:

■ **The editors prefer to go cyber.** Did the Internet kill the SASE? E-mail has become a fast and efficient way to send rejections and acceptances. "I do find it easier to e-mail a response and I like receiving queries via e-mail also," says Susan Pennell, editor of *Collectibles Canada*. "Then I can start a dialogue with the writer until we work out an angle for an article appropriate for my magazine." Dick Baumer, vice president and general manager at Imagination Publishing, says that even if he receives a print submission with a SASE, he finds it easier to respond by e-mail. (So include an e-mail address on any snail-mailed proposals!)

■ **SASEs are to editors as socks are to the dryer.** Editors, for the most part, are human — and as humans, they sometimes do things like drop SASEs behind the coffee machine or separate them from their queries. Diana once sent for *Glamour*'s writers' guidelines, and received a form rejection letter in her SASE. Talk about being knee-capped at the gate!

■ **You screwed up.** When postal rates went up, editors at *Storyteller, Canada's Short Story Magazine* had to contend with SASEs with insufficient postage. "For the first time, we took a close look at those envelopes," says editor Melanie Fogel. The results were discouraging. Common snafus included discrepancies between the address on the cover letter and that on the SASE; an illegible address on the SASE; insufficient postage; and no postage at all. Some writers claimed in their cover letter to have enclosed a SASE but the SASE was nowhere to be found, and other SASEs were returned to the magazine because the writer moved with no forwarding address.

So the question remains: Should you follow the advice in all those writers' books and send a SASE with your query?

Despite the sad response rate for SASEs, some writers and editors insist that the SASE is the way to go. "It seems like the right thing to do, like hand-writing thank you notes and wearing pantyhose even on really hot days," says freelance writer Mary Kennedy. And freelancer Simone Carter says that she would rather spend 50 or 60 cents for an envelope and stamp and have the editorial staff toss it than risk offending an editor.

In the other camp are the stalwart SASE opponents. Some writers decry the cost of the SASE habit. "I send simultaneous submissions to regional parenting publications," says freelance writer Renée Heiss. "With so many manuscripts going out at once, it is not cost-effective to include a SASE with each one. I tell the editors to e-mail me if they are interested so I can send them an electronic copy. That saves me money and saves them time."

Other writers contend that the SASE is a dead giveaway of an amateur. "In what other business does one include an SASE with a proposal?" asks Arnold Howard, editor of *Martial Arts Professional.* "A SASE indicates that the writer is too shy to follow up the written query with a phone call." And Evan Harvey of Careerbuilder.com thinks that the SASE may indicate a stubborn adherence to publishing rules of the past.

Our take on the whole SASE/no SASE debate? It depends on your comfort level with ambiguity. Eric recently sent out a bunch of queries without SASEs. The result? It drove him crazy. When he didn't hear back from a magazine, he wondered whether they didn't want his idea, they hadn't read it yet, or they never received it. If you're the kind of person who needs to know the fate of every query, we suggest including a SASE, keeping in mind that you still may not get the courtesy of a response. If you don't care, don't bother.

If you choose not to send a SASE, however, you don't have to leave a response totally up to fate – request that the editor respond to your e-mail address (however, whether she'll do that or not is anybody's guess), and remember that you can always follow up with a phone call (see, "Never call an editor," p. 68).

You can also downscale your SASE: Try a self-addressed

stamped postcard (SASP) instead. You can preprint your SASPs with options that the editor can check off, such as "Thanks but no thanks," "We're keeping your submission on file," and the ever optimistic, "We're seriously considering your submission and will get back to you by (insert date)." Then stick on postage while grinning with glee in the knowledge that postcards require less postage than letters, and mail your proposal out. "I really like SASPs," says Nancy LePatourel, editor-in-chief of *Oxygen* magazine. "All I have to do is check a box and toss it in the mail."

Of course, the ongoing SASE or no SASE discussion is moot once you've made the decision to work electronically. That means all of your queries are sent via e-mail: no SASE required. But even then, you often won't get a response, and in those cases you'll need to bite the bullet and call the editor.

RULE: If you don't hear anything about your query, assume the magazine doesn't want it and move on.

Just as SASEs get lost or misplaced, so do queries. Call or e-mail the editor to find out the status of your query if you haven't heard back within a certain time period, say four to six weeks — just don't make it two hours. When Linda was starting out, she sent a query to a career magazine and didn't hear back for two months. When she called to follow up, the editor told her that he had never received her query — and that the publishing group had started a new magazine that would be a perfect home for her story. Success! If Linda had given up on the query, she would never have made that sale.

Eric has also learned not to let his queries die a quiet death in the hands of editors. Whenever he sends a query to *GAMES* via e-mail or snail mail, he gets no response — even though he's written a half-dozen pieces for the mag. He waits a few weeks, calls the editor, and often ends up getting the assignment by phone. Why doesn't the editor respond to the queries if they're good enough to warrant an assignment? We have no idea, but Eric has gotten smart to the editor's modus operandi and scored many dollars.

Other potential reasons your query has gone unanswered:

■ **The staff is too busy.** If you think you have a problem with deadlines, imagine trying to put out an entire magazine – every thirty days! The stress of the publishing world can cause major query response delays. "Writers should understand that the stuffing of SASEs is a low-priority job," says Melanie Fogel, editor of *Storyteller, Canada's Short Story Magazine*. "It's done quickly, without much attention to detail, so that we can spend more time on the work we'll be publishing."

■ **The staff is nonexistent.** Sometimes there's just no one to get the job done, which means your query is sitting in a to-be-answered pile somewhere in the editorial office. "We're a small association; I don't have an editorial assistant here and don't expect to get one anytime soon," says Cindy Sweeney, editor of *Dimensions* magazine. "I respond to queries as quickly as I can, but unfortunately I don't have time to make them a priority."

■ **The economy stinks.** A mushy economy means that editors are more careful about handing out assignments, which can leave your query languishing in a pile of unread submissions. "There's a definite relationship between the speed of acceptance and the overall financial outlook for publishers," says Evan Harvey, editor of Careerbuilder.com. "You don't want to commit $400 to an article that may be worth $200 in a month."

■ **Your query is on file.** Sometimes, an AWOL response spells good news for the writer, because it means your query is still under consideration. "Often, when a writer doesn't receive a reply from me it means I'm still holding the query in my 'maybe' file," says Susan Pennell of *Collectibles Canada*. Daniel Kehrer, editor of *Emerging Business*, operates under the same M.O. "I have things that have sat in my file for a year or more that I've eventually purchased," he says. "I think there's a lot of material that ultimately falls into that kind of twilight zone at a lot of publications."

RULE: Check *Writer's Market* for the name of the editor to query.

By the time *Writer's Market* hits the shelves, many of the publications they list have had staff changes. Pick up a copy six months after it hits the shelves, and you can bet that most editors listed are no longer at that publication or in that same position. And here's something even scarier. We have it on good authority that some magazines supply *Writer's Market* with made-up contact names. Why would they do something so deceptive, you ask? So the magazines can tell who hasn't done their research, that's why. Any queries that come in with the *Writer's Market* contact name go right into the recycling bin.

Checking the masthead (the section in the front of the magazine that lists the staff) ups the odds of finding the right editor to target. However, magazines are prepared months ahead of time, so this may also be inaccurate. Your best bet: Spring for the quarter and call the editorial department. You can find a magazine's telephone number in the masthead, in *Writer's Market*, or on the publication's website. Don't be shy about this. Most likely, when you call you will reach the editorial voicemail. If they have one of those systems where you can dial a staff member by name, dial in the name of the editor you wanted to query to make sure she's still there (you can also do this after hours if you don't want to risk having the editor pick up the phone). If the phone system doesn't offer this option, leave a message asking for the name of the person you should query for an article on such-and-such. If you're too scared to talk to the editor you're thinking of pitching, call an editorial assistant. They're usually pretty pleasant and will often give you helpful information.

Sometimes you'll get a human being on the line. Rarely, you'll reach the actual person you want to query. And even more rarely, that editor will ask you to pitch your idea over the phone. You may want to practice pitching your idea in less than 30 seconds so that you don't sound like a wuss.

RULE: You have to query to get an assignment.

With many magazines, especially small and online publications, an impressive introduction letter will open the door to new assignments. Diana sent the editor of a trade magazine for IT (information technology) contractors an e-mail about her technical writing background and asking whether he needed freelancers. The editor wrote back to request her resumé and clips. A month later, he wrote to assign her an article at a buck a word, and for two years, she had an assignment from the publication nearly every month – usually major features and cover stories.

Linda has a template introduction letter she uses mainly for online magazines. When she learns about a new magazine, she pastes the letter into the body of an e-mail message, changes details where necessary to reflect the magazine she's writing to, and sends it off. Almost every online magazine she's written for was approached this way. Here's the letter she sends:

> Dear Ms. Hireme:
>
> I enjoyed the Boring Business Magazine website!
>
> Do you need a business writer? As a freelance writer based in the Boston area, I've written for more than 100 magazines, including such business publications as eCommerce Business, Wired, Entrepreneur's Business Start-Ups, and Nation's Business, and such non-business magazines as Men's Fitness, Psychology Today, and Redbook. I also wrote irreverent marketing columns for 1099 magazine (www.1099.com, "Getting Work") and Entrepreneur's HomeOfficeMag.com. You can see a full list of published articles, editor testimonials, and clips at www.twowriters.net.

Chapter 3 - No-Fear Querying

Thanks for taking the time to check out my clips and credentials. I look forward to discussing with you how my skills can benefit Boring Business Magazine!

Best regards,
Linda Formichelli

Also, there's no need to rack your brain to come up with ideas to query trade mags, no matter what the other books or magazine articles say. If you have an idea to query, go ahead and query it, but know that it's not difficult to be invited into a trade magazine editor's stable of freelancers with a simple introduction letter. Trade magazines usually have their editorial calendars scheduled a year in advance, so they know exactly what they're going to cover and when they're going to cover it. Moreover, trades are plugged into the industry they cover; rarely will they meet a freelancer over the transom who knows their readership better than they do. They usually have files full of great ideas, and their only problem is finding the writers to report and write interesting copy.

Linda has written for dozens of trades, and she's never proposed a single original idea to them – except that they should give her an assignment. Once she sent her intro letter to 24 trades and received eight assignments within the next two weeks! Eric has landed articles with more than a dozen trades with his introduction letter. Here's the letter he uses:

Dear Mr. Bigshot:

I enjoyed the Noodle Maker Fortnightly website!

Do you assign articles to freelance writers? As a writer based in the Boston area, I've written for dozens of trade magazines, including Indian Gaming Business, In-Plant Graphics, and Modern Reprographics. I've also written for such non-trades as GAMES, Psychology Today, and Woman's Day.

May I send you some clips?

Best regards,
W. Eric Martin

If you don't have any publishing credits yet, find trade magazines that relate to your job or hobby and tout your impressive credentials in your letter. You can find trades for every (and we mean every) industry or hobby. Case in point: Linda recently read an announcement for a new trade magazine dealing in dung management. And when Diana wrote advertising copy for a bandage manufacturer, she subscribed to *Journal of Burn Care and Rehabilitation.*

Whether you're writing to trades or newsstand magazines, if you're sending an e-mail, use an attention-grabbing subject line. For example, Eric's subject line will read, "Writer for Woman's Day, GAMES, Psychology Today, & more." If you don't have a lot of writing credits yet, do what another freelance writer does: Use the subject line "Do you need a business (health, kids', etc.) writer?"

Sometimes you can even skip the query letter process with a major publication. Freelancer Jennie Phipps landed her first consumer magazine piece simply by sending a note to a magazine for a reader-participation feature. One of the editors liked what she read and called. Phipps told her about her background and gave her some ideas, and as a result, she got an assignment and has been writing for the publication for six years. "I think having good ideas and being able to demonstrate that you can write them is the only thing that's important," she says.

Not that every communication you send in to a magazine will generate such interest, but this story does fall under the category of "You never know who's reading the mail."

RULE: Never call an editor.

Forget query letters and e-mail. Many writers land assignments with moxie and a phone call. Take Elissa Sonnenberg, for instance. When she got a form rejection from a national glossy, she called the editor to try to change his mind. "The point of my calling an editor of a great magazine for which I aspired to write was to establish a rapport with the guy, to become something more than a name on a letter he could easily reject," she says. "So I asked him why he rejected my idea and made some small talk, until I laughingly told him I thought he made a mistake in rejecting my story idea." The editor laughed, too – and gave her the assignment.

But you don't have to wait for a rejection to land in your mailbox before calling an editor. When Diana was starting out, she noticed that her local chain of weekly newspapers published an endless stream of feature articles written by freelancers. The subjects were usually bridal, parenting, and gardening – the types of stories Diana wanted to write. So during her lunch break (she was still working full-time) she called the newspaper's main office and asked for the assigning editor. When she got her on the phone, she quickly pushed her credentials and asked for an assignment. And guess what? The editor, who was not at all perturbed about taking a phone call, asked Diana to fax over her résumé and clips, then gave her two assignments the next day! Diana eventually became an ongoing feature correspondent for the newspaper until she gave up the gig for higher paying assignments. If you want to write for a local paper or small newsstand magazine, we say go for it. Even major newspapers like *The Boston Globe* or the *Los Angeles Times* can be receptive to a quick phone call. With their crazy schedules, it's easier for a newspaper editor to give you a quick "yea" or "nay" than to slog through your query letter.

This tactic works best with newspapers and smaller magazines, but we say hats off to you if you can sell to a glossy newsstand magazine with a phone call! Writer Bethanne Kelly Patrick says, "Almost all of my best assignments have started with a telephone conversation. This works for me because I am glib and loquacious! Often I'll call an editor just to say, 'Hi, this is who I am and I'd like to know about your query process' – or I'll ask a specific question about the process that wasn't covered in any of the guidelines I found." She'll then follow up with an e-mail or a snail-mailed package of clips. And Patrick will keep calling until she achieves her goal: an assignment.

Patrick set up a phone appointment with one website editor after he'd seen her clips. He blew off that call, but she still wouldn't take no for an answer. "I called infrequently and at odd times, not enough to seem like a stalker or a pest, but enough to keep my name on his radar screen," she says. Finally, eight weeks after their initial conversation, the editor put Patrick in touch with the site's managing editor, who was having trouble finding good writers. She loved Patrick's clips and sent her contracts for two assignments within a few days. Patrick has been working for her ever since.

You can also use the phone for follow-ups. If you sent a query and haven't received a response in a reasonable amount of time (at least a month), it's perfectly okay to call and ask about the status of your proposal. Call the editor and say something like, "On September 20, I sent you a query for an article called 'Please Hire Me.' I haven't heard back from you, so I'm calling to make sure you received it." When Linda called an editor at *Rosie* to follow up on a query she'd sent two months ago, the editor said she'd never seen the query, asked Linda to describe her idea, asked her to tell her about herself, and told her to fax the query to her directly. (The editor then advised Rosie O'Donnell to shut down the magazine to eliminate any possibility of encountering this "Linda" character again. Now you know the real story behind the demise of *Rosie*.)

If you reach the editor instead of his voice mail, be prepared to pitch the idea over the phone if he asks you to. Linda learned this the hard way when an editor at *Ladies' Home Journal* said, "Tell me about your idea." Caught by surprise, Linda stuttered for a bit and finally managed to blurt out a few descriptive sentences.

Don't worry about all that advice you read that you should never call the editor. If you're smart enough to pick up this book, we're pretty sure you're not some slobbering idiot who's going to call an editor to shoot the breeze or pitch a story about the sex life of frogs to a home decorating magazine. Magazine editors are human beings, not rapacious writer-eating fiends. If you're courteous, professional, and quick to the point, they won't hang up on you – we promise. *Shape*'s editor-in-chief Anne Russell says that she recently got a phone pitch from a writer who had a "hot story" about a championship boogie boarder. "It was totally wrong for us," she says, "but I have to give her credit that she called from Chile."

Then there's the flip side. Many writers we know admit to getting sweaty when an editor calls them – to offer an assignment, at that! What's with this fear of the phone? Whether you're afraid of initiating a call, or terrified of answering, you need to get over this fear – fast. As freelance writer Jennie Phipps reminds us, "Being a freelance writer means being a salesperson as much as 50 percent of the time. Good salespeople know how to work the phones. Good freelance writers have to learn how to do it, too."

RULE: You need to be timely.

Time is relative in the magazine world, and timely doesn't mean "right now." In July, what are all editors vetting during staff meetings? If you said patriotic articles, go to the back of the class. Most magazines work six to nine months ahead, which means they filled their Fourth of July issue by January. When Eric e-mailed a Valentine's Day idea to his *Woman's Day* editor in September, he was told that they were already wrapping up the March issue!

Get a cheap wall calendar and set it six to nine months ahead. Come May or June, when you're looking at the calendar, you'll be reminded that it's time to start brainstorming for Christmas ideas, and in March you'll see that it's not the time for pieces on Easter egg decorating tips, but for articles on how to carve the perfect Jack-o-lantern.

Diana keeps a "tickle file." Like most people, she gets her best ideas while in the thick of things. Last year, for example, she had to plan a couple of holiday gatherings right after her son was born, which gave her a good story idea for a parenting magazine. She wrote the idea down and stuck it into a file marked

"February." When February rolled around, she had this and a handful of other holiday-focused ideas to pitch to her editors.

Need ideas to stick in your file? National holidays are always a great tie in. Every month is chock full of holidays you can glean ideas from, such as Organize Your Home Day and National Pet Week. Check out websites such as www.earthcalendar.net for other holidays you probably haven't heard of that can lead to great article ideas.

RULE: Write your query according "The Formula."

It has been drummed into our heads that every pitch should include the hook, the pitch, the body, the creds, and the close – in that order. But sometimes "The Formula" gets a little stale. Why not start your query with a compelling quote from one of your sources? Or stick your credentials in the first paragraph, especially if you're trying to sell yourself to the editor versus your idea? For example, whenever Linda pitches an article about stopping spam, junk faxes, or telemarketing, she mentions up front that she's the creator and co-owner of BadAds.org, a website about intrusive advertising. When Diana pitches to technology magazines, the first thing she tells the editor is that she's a former technical writer who worked in the IT field. This sets her apart from writers who don't know Java from JavaScript. For another query to a women's magazine, she started off by mentioning some of the magazines she has written for because she'd learned that this editor liked to work with writers who'd "been around the block."

Another idea: If you've written for the magazine before, you can start off by reminding the editor how well received your article was by readers. For example, when Linda queried *Nation's Business* for an article about business travel, she used this lead-in:

My article on micromanagement in the November 1997 issue of Nation's Business seems to have hit a nerve in small business owners: I was interviewed on the topic for the radio show "Small Business Focus," gave a talk at a Chamber of Commerce, and have had several trade magazines ask me to write about micromanagement for their industries. Here's a query for another article I think will have a strong impact among your readers.

As you can see, you don't need to stick to the same old same old when writing your query. Be creative! Let your personality show! That's what most editors are looking for anyway.

RULE: Send your query to the managing editor/the articles editor/the janitor/etc.

Check out these mastheads from two different magazines.

Thomas Kunkel
President

Rem Rieder
Editor and Senior Vice President

Lissa Reynolds
Art Director

Lori Robertson
Managing Editor

Jill Rosen
Assistant Managing Editor

Kathryn S. Wenner
Associate Editor

**Christopher Callahan,
Carl Sessions Stepp**
Senior Editors

Susan Paterno, Sherry Ricchiardi
Senior Writers

**Nina J. Easton, Lucinda Fleeson,
Kelly Heyboer, Jane Kirtley,
Charles Layton, Mark Lisheron,
John Morton, Barb Palser,
Deborah Potter, Rachel Smolkin,
Sharyn Vane**
Contributing Writers

**Andrea Cohen, Carla Correa,
Michael Duck, Luciana Lopez,
Sarah Schaffer**
Editorial Assistants

Poets&Writers
POETS & WRITERS MAGAZINE

Editor
THERESE EIBEN

Deputy Editor
MARY GANNON

Managing Editor
JIM ANDREWS

Associate Editor
KEVIN LARIMER

Art Direction
MURRAY GREENFIELD

Contributing Editors
CAROLYN T. HUGHES
JOANNA SMITH RAKOFF

Advertising Director
SHOSHANNA WINGATE

Advertising Associate
JOSHUA MANDELBAUM

Advertising Assistant
MARCUS KRAUSE

Circulation Director
PAULA COLLINS

Managing editor, assistant managing editor, associate editor, deputy editor, senior editor…you can go bonkers trying to figure out who does what. Making a habit of always sending your queries to, say, the managing editor can get you in trouble. The managing editor at one magazine may be the editor who calls all the shots, while at another magazine, the articles editor runs the show. And with smaller magazines, it's not uncommon to find the editor-in-chief panning through the slush pile for freelancer gold.

At times it's easy to figure out who should receive your missive. If you're pitching a story on the latest advances in lice control and your target publication lists a "health editor," *voila*! But don't sit around scratching your noggin if you're confused – pick up the phone, call the magazine, and ask whom you should send your proposal to. If you're too much of a wimp to do that, then it's a safe bet to send your query to an editorial assistant. She'll get it where it needs to go, and may be flattered that you trusted your gem to her.

RULE: Don't e-mail your query unless you've worked with the editor before.

Many a writer has landed an assignment by zapping off a query via e-mail when they were lucky enough to get their hands on an editor's e-mail address. In fact, that's our M.O. If we see that a magazine's e-mail addresses are always formulated as, say, firstname.lastname@magazine.com, we'll figure out our target editor's e-mail address and shoot off our queries. Other times, we find an e-mail address on the magazine's website. Sometimes we get an editor's e-mail address from a friend, usually with the warning, "Don't tell my editor where you got her e-mail address!" Usually, the editor responds with a nice reply; we know of no writers who have been interrogated by an editor about how they divined her e-mail address!

Diana sends e-mail queries almost exclusively. She has never had an editor admonish her for making first contact this way, even if the editor hasn't made her e-mail address public. The way Diana sees it, a strong proposal is a strong proposal, and since editors complain about getting so few of them, why would they be upset if one comes through e-mail? Should an editor throw a hissy fit over an e-mailed pitch, Diana would see this as a sign from the gods that this editor is probably someone she avoid at all costs because of the PITA factor.

E-mail queries are not only acceptable but are *de rigueur* for tech and online magazines, who often turn up their noses at mailed queries. Linda broke in with e-mailed queries and introductions to such techie pubs as *Wired News, eCommerce Business,* and *Techtarget.* Diana cracked *The Next Big Thing, 1099,* and *Contract Professional* with e-mail pitches.

RULE: Come up with ideas to pitch to editors.

It can be even better to ask the editor what she's looking for and then pitch that. Diana had lunch with two of her editors at sister technical publications, and they spent a half-hour listing all the stories they wanted to do in the future. Diana sat there and took copious notes. Linda recently asked her editor at *Woman's Day* what she was looking for and received a list of ideas via e-mail. Editors will sometimes also use this opportunity to tell you about changes in the magazine such as new sections you can target. It doesn't hurt to ask.

However, this works only with editors you've written for before; editors don't have time to give hot tips and insider information to every writer who wants to break in. "More established writers, and those I've worked with, will e-mail or call me to talk about what subjects we're interested in," says Denise Foley of *Prevention.* "I don't return phone calls from people I don't know – I'm not being rude, I just don't have the time."

If you've got an especially supportive networking group, you can ask your peers to share this kind of information. Recently, Linda received an e-mail from one of her editors at a women's magazine who was desperate for story ideas in certain areas, which she outlined in her letter. Linda passed this information to several writers in her network, who then were able to target their pitches based on this editor's need.

RULE: Putting a deadline in your query will ensure a quicker response.

Good luck with that! The reason it can take so long to get a response is not because the editor is taking her time carefully contemplating your query for two months – it's because your query is sitting underneath a pile of hundreds of other proposals from other writers. Your deadline could come and go without an editor ever having set eyes on your query – and when she finally does get to it, she may toss it in the bin because that date you insisted upon is long past.

Your deadline may also give the editor the idea that you're dying to circulate the query to other pubs – not a good thing. "A deadline would tell me he was going to offer it to my competition, which would mean that he and we are likely to soon part," says Brian Alm, editor of *Rental Management Magazine*. "I am selfish with the few writers I use. I spend a lot of time teaching them about the industry and working over story plans with them. I do not expect to see them take all that knowledge and grooming to the other magazines in the industry, and have their byline show up there after I have made them known in this industry." Yikes!

Now, if you have an idea that will go stale fast, feel free to write something like, "Because this is a timely topic, if I don't hear from you by [five seconds from now, October 1, whatever], I'll assume you're not interested in the story." It won't guarantee a faster response, but it will allow you to circulate the query to other editors guilt-free. (Unless you, like Linda, are a proponent of the simultaneous query – in which case it won't matter at all.)

RULE: Tell the editor how long it will take to write the article.

Many books and articles on querying suggest that you put in your proposal, "I can have 'My Great Article' finished in three weeks." We guess the writer's underlying assumption is that the editor is going to say something like, "Wow, three weeks! The idea is just okay, but the delivery date can't be beat. I'll take it!" Fat chance. And what if the editors at this magazine like to have their articles in two-and-a-half weeks, or they like to give writers two months to ensure well-researched pieces?

If you're lucky enough to land the assignment, your editor will tell you what her deadline is. "I'm more interested in knowing whether the writer can work within my schedule," says Suma CM, senior director of online content for Jungle Media Group, the publishers of *MBA Jungle*.

By stating a finish date, you may be pulling yourself out of the game before it starts. "[It's] not a make-or-break issue normally, but it could be," says Alm. "If the writer has no background in my industry and claims he can produce 1,000 words in three weeks on an esoteric or difficult topic that is very industry-specific, I know he's blowing smoke and doesn't know himself well enough to trust."

RULE: Be familiar with the magazine before querying it.

Guess what? Even this rule can be broken, although editors will probably put a price on our heads for saying so. In fact, Linda's first assignment was for a magazine she found listed in *Writer's Market*; she had never actually seen the magazine before she queried. If you don't believe us, maybe you'll believe these writers who have sold ideas to magazines they've never read:

My first two writing assignments were from magazines that I had never heard of, let alone read. In fact, the second writing assignment was with a magazine that I couldn't get a copy of even after I had landed the assignment. The first time I read the magazine was when they sent me my complimentary copy after publishing my story in their publication.

I think with both of these articles the thing that hooked the editor was that I was offering a completely different view on their topic. I had no preconceived ideas about what should go in the magazine, and just queried with what I wanted to write about.

—Freelance writer Liz Palmer

I'm almost embarrassed to say that I wrote an article for the official "Babylon Five" magazine having never watched the show or read the mag. It's not something I'd recommend, but it got me a nice paycheck.

Basically, I had interviewed an actor named Robin Sachs and during the interview I found out that he had appeared in "Babylon Five" a number of times, so I pitched the interview to the magazine. They wanted it, but they wanted it skewed toward his experiences on the show, of course. At the time I had no idea that the show was full of different kinds of aliens with a variety of agendas and it was very complicated.

I survived by hitting up my Internet friends until I found one who watched the show regularly. He gave me a crash course and the article was a winner!

—Freelance writer Cynthia Boris

I have written for several magazines without ever having seen them, mainly parenting regionals outside of my region, such as Atlanta Baby and Minnesota Parent. As far as I'm concerned – and this could be completely inaccurate – they all seem to be very similar in their content needs. I've also written for a couple of subscription-only e-pubs that I had never seen. In one particular case, I knew the one assistant editor rather well, and she gave me more details about what they wanted than were in the guidelines, so that was very helpful.

—Freelance writer Lisa Beamer

I've written for a magazine I've never read. The Canadian Writer's Journal carried a market listing for NeWest Review, *which stated that they covered politics and entertainment for West Canada. I pitched them a story about housing shortages in British Columbia.*

Little did I know that they focused solely on the Canadian Prairie provinces. They accepted my query anyway on the condition that I tailored it towards people moving from the prairie provinces to BC. It was my first sale!

– Freelance writer James D. Thwaites

If you can't find a magazine on the stands but you've read the guidelines or its listing in *Writer's Market,* you can usually get a pretty good idea of what the editors are looking for. Besides that, if you can't find a magazine on the newsstand, that means it's probably not a very big publication – and it may be much easier to break into. Editors might not like the idea of a writer querying a magazine he's never read, but in the competitive world of free-lance writing, speed and efficiency are what it's all about. The more you query, the more work you get. All it costs you is a SASE or SASP for the possibility of an assignment – free if you use e-mail or have ditched these (see page 60) – so why not take the risk?

Still want to read the magazine before querying, but you can't find it anywhere? Write to the magazine requesting their guide-lines and asking how you can get a sample issue of the magazine (include a SASE). Many publications will send you a copy for free. If not, they'll tell you how much it costs to order a copy from them. You can also check out the articles in back issues through online databases (see "Database access is expensive," p. 99).

However, if you can find the magazine on any newsstand, you really should take a look at it. "A lot of freelancers are lazy," says *Shape*'s Anne Russell. "They won't spend $3.99 to do some mar-ket research that will help them tailor their pitch." For example, Russell regularly fields pitches for 3,000-word profiles of profes-sional sportswomen. "It's clear that these writers haven't even looked at our magazine," she says. "We don't do 3,000-word profiles." Considering that a magazine in this league probably gets hundreds of pitches every week, you're probably writing yourself a rejection if you don't check out the magazine before sending a query.

RULE: Make sure your query letter is perfect before sending it out.

No, we're not saying you should decorate your letterhead with sticky coffee rings or skip the spell check. Your queries should be as pristine as possible, and your quotes and stats accurate. But we know too many writers who get hung up on the picayune details of their proposals, which either takes the juice out of their writing or prevents them from sending their work out at all.

Perfectionism is deadly and we think it kills more beginning writing careers than grammar accidents and etiquette gaffes. Diana almost fell victim to this pernicious plague, but through self-help and experience, she's nearly eradicated perfectionism from her writing life. She studied other, more successful, freelancers and watched how they worked. They didn't fret for days over a query; they did the best they could and got the work out there. Diana began keeping a file of all the wonderful things her editors said to her about her writing and her work habits, and whenever

Diana's Query Checklist

☐ Double check editor's name

☐ Double check address

☐ Make sure name in address matches name in salutation

☐ References to magazine correct?

☐ Read aloud twice!

☐ Clips enclosed?

☐ Let sit overnight

☐ 2nd set of eyes proofread

☐ READ ONCE MORE BEFORE SENDING

she began to feel paralyzed by the need to be perfect, she'd take those notes out and relish them. She also keeps a checklist handy and uses it before sending a query out to ensure she's using the right editor name and address.

The best cure, however, is to just do it. No obsessing, no worrying. Write the darn thing, let it rest, proof it, and hit the "send" button or pop the query in the mail.

Shape's Anne Russell understands that even the best writers make mistakes, and this usually comes about because the writer is trying too hard. She, in fact, has done it herself with her own correspondence. "I'll run back to grab the letter from the outbox, convinced that I've misspelled a person's name," she says. "Your brain starts playing tricks on you." Her solution? Let the query sit for a day, and when you come back to it, the errors will glare at you. "It's like buying a gun. There should be a waiting period before you send your queries out," she says.

Even if after all your efforts a mistake does rear its ugly head in your query, it doesn't have to be a dealbreaker. Both Diana and Linda have sold to major newsstand magazines with queries that were missing words in the first sentences. An entire word! In the very first sentence! And once Linda put a query for Magazine X into the envelope addressed to Magazine Y. The query was rejected, but Linda also got a very nice note from the editor assuring her that such mistakes are common and forgivable.

Many times we've seen panicked posts from writers on on-line bulletin boards who wonder if they should call editors to fess up to boo-boos in their query. We say, "DON'T!" Three-quarters of the time, an editor isn't going to notice a missing word or a typo, especially if the rest of the letter shines. And if they do notice it, most editors will forgive a minor editorial transgression. Calling attention to it makes you appear insecure and anal. Russell agrees: "You'll just appear to be a complete psycho." Consider it a learning experience, hope the editor doesn't notice, and move on to your next query.

On the other hand, Russell is not so forgiving of major mistakes. She finds it offensive when a writer misspells her name ("I have a very simple name") and woe to the writer who sends her query to the magazine's subscription processing center ("It happens more than you would imagine.") When she was an editor at *Working Woman*, Russell read a query that included, "And I know dentists will love this article." Clearly, the writer of this gem sent out queries willy nilly, hoping for any old bite. All these things are dealbreakers for her – and many other editors, too – so if you've made this kind of mistake, don't bother apologizing. In Russell's words, "You've blown it."

But there is a bright side: with editors getting so much mail, rarely will they remember that you were the writer who misspelled Mississippi in your query letter!

RULE: Your goal is to land a big assignment with your query.

Several things can happen with a great query. You may get the assignment to write your story – or the editor may reject your idea, but be so impressed with your writing that she assigns you her own idea. A query that doesn't sell an idea can still showcase your writing and get your name in front of the editor, and therefore lead to big bucks.

Brian Alm of *Rental Management* has rejected queries but given the writers of these queries assignments from his own pile of ideas based on the writers' obvious talent. "And a number of times I have taken the query and revised the assignment the writer had proposed into something specific to our industry, with quotes and industry interviews and examples, and paid the writer twice what he had originally asked for in order to have this exclusivity," says Alm. Denise Foley of *Prevention* has also invited writers of rejected queries into her stable. "Absolutely! Several of our regular freelancers came to us that way," she says.

So while it's true that your main goal is to sell an article on the topic you're querying, keep an open mind if the editor rejects the idea but asks for additional clips, or if she calls you with another topic to write about.

Chapter **Four**

Signing on the Dotted Line
Renegades Get Fatter, Fairer, Safer Contracts

Many contracts are pure evil: They gobble up all the rights to the articles you've sweated over, put you in the hot seat should some psycho sue the magazine, and give the magazine the right to pay you a fraction of what you're owed if the editors change their minds about your article for any reason. Don't throw a hissyfit – rebel! Here's how you can make contracts work for you.

RULE: The contract is set in stone.

When it's a buyer's market, the buyer gets to set the terms. That means writers rarely sit in the catbird seat, unless your name happens to rhyme with "Even Thing." Many editors automatically hand writers the contract their lawyers wrote up for them – the contract that makes writers cry over its onerous terms. Most writers wipe their eyes and resignedly sign the contract, so editors aren't compelled to make it more writer-friendly.

If, however, the writer has the temerity to ask for changes, the editor may be happy to make them. Although the publisher may have more leverage with contracts, it doesn't mean you have to roll over and play dead.

A clause you may want to ask about is the one that gives the magazine all rights to the article. (You might encounter all-rights contracts under the term "work-for-hire"; since the publisher owns all rights, including the copyright, you're nothing more than a hired gun.) If you think the article has reprint value, tell your editor you'd like to give them First North American Serial Rights, where the magazine gets the right to be the first to print the article in North America. If that's a no go, you may be able to get the editor to agree to "non-exclusive rights," which allows the magazine to reprint the article in its sister publications or sell it to a content provider, but still gives you the right to sell it to other magazines.

Also, angle for extra money if the magazine insists on electronic rights along with print rights. For publication on a website, the National Writers Union suggests a level commensurate with first print rights. For other electronic rights, the NWU suggests between 30 and 50 percent of the first print rights fee for use of the writer's work in a single electronic outlet.

Another clause to change is the one where the writer guarantees that the article breaks no laws anywhere in the known universe. The clause goes something like this:

> *Author represents and warrants that any article Author may present under this Agreement shall be Author's wholly original work, not previously published in any media, in whole or in part; that the work will not infringe any person's or entity's copyright, trademarks, service mark, or other proprietary rights, and will not constitute defamation, invasion of the rights of privacy, or infringement of any other rights of any kind of any third party. In the event that any threat, demand, claim, or action is asserted against Magazine X or any of its affiliates, or their officers, directors, or employees, by any person or entity alleging copyright, trademark, or service mark infringement; unfair competition; misuse of proprietary ideas or expression; defamation; invasion of privacy; or any other claim arising out of Magazine X's publication of Author's article, Author shall defend, indemnify and hold*

*harmless Magazine X, its affiliates, and their officers, direc-
tors, and employees from any and all liabilities, expenses, costs,
damages, settlements, or judgements, including attorney fees,
incurred in connection with such threat, demand, claim or
action if Author is shown to have violated his agreements as
judged in a court of law.*

How are you supposed to know if you're infringing on the
trademark of some obscure business in Botswana? Ask that this
onerous clause be removed, or at a minimum insist that the phrase
"to the best of the author's knowledge," be added, as in, "The
author warrants to the best of her knowledge that any article
Author may present under this agreement…"

And if your editor is having a good day, you can add some
clauses of your own. After talking with her sister-in-law, an independent consultant, about how contracts work in other industries,
Diana considered adding a clause to all future contracts that reads,
"Payments made net 10 receive 1 percent discount." What that
means is if the publisher issues you a check within 10 days of the
invoice date, they can lop off one percent of the total invoice.
Hey, Diana's willing to take a one percent pay cut for the privilege
of fast cash. Such invoice discount schemes are common in the
business world, and the magazine's printer probably offers such a
discount for prompt payers *and* interest fees on delinquent
accounts. Why shouldn't writers follow suit?

RULE: You're getting the contract all the writers get.

If an editor sends you a rights-grabby contract, calmly call him
and say, "I'd like the other contract, please." We know many magazines have two contracts – the rapacious one they foist on new,
inexperienced writers that asks them to sign away the rights to
everything except the clothes they're wearing, and the one that is
more reasonable. Unless you like being degraded, you want the
reasonable one. It helps if you can do a little homework before

you get to the contract stage with a magazine. Check around with your network, or if you belong to an online magazine writing community like Freelance Success or Freelance Online (see Appendix 12, p. 196), ask whether any of the members have worked for the magazine before and what kind of contract they signed. That way if the editor tells you they don't have "another contract," you can say with some authority, "That's interesting, because I know of several other writers who got that other contract." The other thing you can say is, "Gee, the contract you gave me is an all-rights contract, and I usually write for magazines that offer a First North American Serial Rights contract," and see if they offer a different contract.

When Eric got an assignment from a gaming magazine, he was unsatisfied with the all-rights terms. He asked whether the editor would buy first rights instead, and the editor quickly faxed him a first-rights contract. The magazine obviously had two contracts on hand, and sent writers the more restrictive one as a matter of course.

RULE: Never sign an all-rights contract.

Many writers make a huge deal about retaining the rights to their articles, but sometimes it's worth it to take the money and run. Both Linda and Diana have signed some pretty awful contracts, and will probably do so in the future if, and only if, we decide the article has no resale value. For example, Diana wrote several columns for a technical publication about job opportunities for software programmers with specific skill sets at a particular time. Since the economy is always in flux and skill sets can go from hot to cold in a matter of months, she knew she wouldn't be able to sell the columns elsewhere. Instead, she traded all rights for a higher per-word pay rate.

RULE: Once you negotiate a contract, that's the one you'll always receive.

Au contraire. Publications can be quite sneaky about changing their contracts. Linda once called an editor because her check, which was due within 30 days of acceptance – according to the contract – was two weeks late. "You're mistaken," said the editor. "We pay on publication." Confused, Linda checked her most recent contract and discovered that the magazine, which was having money problems, had stealthily changed the contract from payment on acceptance to pay-on-publication – without telling Linda about the change. The moral of the story: Read *every* contract, even if you've worked for the magazine dozens of times already, and question your editor about any changes that look unsavory.

RULE: Editors don't like talking about money.

The truth is, most *writers* don't like talking about money. We'd rather ask about word counts and due dates, and avoid asking the really important question: "How much do you pay and when can I expect my check?" But it's in your best interest to talk dollars up front. Nothing is more discouraging than going through the whole assignment rigmarole and discovering that your editor offers all new writers to the magazine the non-negotiable rate of three cents per word under a work-for-hire contract. The only way you can make an informed decision on whether to accept an assignment is to ask the editor about pay *before* she launches into her spiel about due dates, word counts, and topic slants. Take our word for it – she won't faint with surprise at your chutzpah.

You can avoid the whole problem altogether by investigating the magazine's pay rates before you send your query. Contact other writers in your network and ask them how they fared with *Sheep! Magazine*. Did the magazine pay promptly? Was the editor willing to budge on a quoted rate? These kinds of questions are more polite than asking, "Yo, how much did you get for that article on sheep health?" A few freelancers will get all shifty eyed and uncomfortable if you ask them a direct question like that – and we're sure Miss Manners would slap your greasy little palm with her fan. But even if they don't offer that information, you can probably figure out whether the magazine is worth approaching by what they *do* tell you. (Linda and Diana, frank talkers that they are, regularly share such monetary matters.)

RULE: You must have a contract.

Let's face it: Contracts are there to protect the magazine, not the lowly writer. For example, many contracts give the magazine all rights to your article. But according to the NWU, if you have no contract, the magazine automatically gets only First North American Serial Rights, meaning that the rights revert back to you after publication and you can sell reprints of the article. And you know that awful clause in many contracts – the one that says that you're legally and financially responsible should a reader of your article sue the magazine for any reason? If you don't have a contract, you don't have that clause.

However, do get a written record of the assignment if the editor doesn't offer you a contract. Save the original assignment letter or e-mail – the one where the editor tells you what the article is about and how much and when you'll get paid. If your editor doesn't volunteer an assignment letter, ask for one or write one up yourself and ask her to approve it. If something does go wrong down the pike, at least you'll have something in writing to fall back on.

RULE: Never accept a pay-on-publication contract.

Imagine this: You find a nice formal outfit at a local clothing store, but instead of whipping out your credit card, you tell the cashier that you'll pay for the suit only should an occasion arise

Chapter 4 - Signing on the Dotted Line

where you actually wear it.

Sounds silly, right? But that's the same situation writers face every day when they're offered assignments from magazines that pay on publication instead of on acceptance. These magazines offer an assignment, accept the article, edit the piece, hold it until print time, publish it – and then, finally, pay the writer. And that's assuming that the magazine doesn't change its editorial focus or go out of business before your article makes it to print.

You can never know whether a magazine pays on publication or on acceptance until you look at its contract; though you'd expect only smaller magazines with little financing to pay on publication, this often isn't the case. "You can't generalize," says Dian Killian, journalism division organizer for the National Writer's Union and director of the Publication Rights Clearinghouse. Websites often pay on publication, but that's because many of them post articles so quickly that it's impossible for them to pay before publication.

Magazine editors offer several reasons for paying on publication instead of on acceptance. Some magazines, for example, are on tight budgets and need time to earn the money to pay writers. "I can accept articles for [my newsletters] in one day that total over one thousand dollars," says Angela Giles Klocke, editor of *The Writing Parent* and *The Writing Child.* "I operate on a shoestring budget and rely on advertising, sales, and my own writing sales to pay writers. There's no way I could pay for all the articles in one lump sum. So I pay once they are published, which leaves me time to then earn that money."

Pay-on-publication is also an easier system for magazines, since they can pay all their writers at once instead of dealing with invoices spread throughout the payment period. "For *Adbusters* – a non-profit mag with a small staff – it is largely a question of practicality," says senior editor James MacKinnon. "We typically hit the 'acceptance' point for most pieces fairly close to deadline anyway, so payment after publication is a simple system that allows us to pay everyone at once and limits the likelihood of error. Being able to pay in a block like this also simplifies our financial workings."

Editors also say that paying on publication gives them more time to guide newbie writers. "Pay-on-pub allows us to work with new and emerging writers, non-journalists, and others outside the professional core of writers," adds MacKinnon. "We often work with people to develop their initial idea, take a new approach, or extensively fine-tune the writing; other magazines would simply dismiss these writers as non-professionals. At what point, in a process like the one just described, is material 'accepted'?"

Finally, there's the CYA aspect; editors don't want to put out money for something they may not be able to use. "In our case, as a custom publisher, we must let our clients approve manuscripts and design, and at any point they could decide to pull something or change something. That almost never happens, but it is an option for them which would leave us with having paid for something we then could not use," says Rebecca Rolfes, senior VP and editorial director for Imagination Publishing. "Kill fees are, of course, part of our contract, but we can't tie up our editorial dollars for articles that clients may want to drop or hold until later."

Editors may have their reasons for pay-on-pub, but that doesn't make it any easier for writers who accept such contracts. After all, as the name implies, if your article never makes it to publication – even through no fault of your own – you won't see one sou (or you'll get stuck with the kill fee). "I was burned by a new publication that insisted on paying only upon publication, but they assured me that they would run my article in a couple of months," says Maureen Dixon, a former freelance magazine writer who now writes public relations materials. "The publication folded – of course – the month my article was slated to run."

Even if the magazine doesn't go belly-up, publication lead times are often six months or more, and that's a long time to wait to get paid. What's more, you can't sell reprints of an article until it's actually been published, which curtails your moneymaking power even more.

That's why both the NWU and ASJA urge writers to reject

pay-on-pub contracts. "We encourage members to negotiate contracts that stipulate payment on acceptance, not publication," says Killian. "Numerous problems can arise otherwise."

On the other hand, if you have enough pay-on-acceptance assignments that you can afford to wait for a check from one magazine, you can profit. Linda, for example, writes regularly for one magazine that pays on publication, and she's never had a problem getting paid.

If you do decide to write for magazines that pay on publication, take these steps to protect yourself:

■ **Negotiate.** Perhaps the magazine will be willing to bend the contract for you – it never hurts to ask. "I always, always negotiate, and it often works," says freelance writer Monique Cuvelier. "I simply explain what an inconvenience it is to have my pay rolling in half a year after I did the work, and that it's my policy to be paid 30 days after submission. It's only fair."

■ **Get a firm date.** If the editor won't change the pay-on-pub terms, perhaps you can get her to include the expected date of publication in the contract so that you have some idea of what your cash flow will look like in the future. Or better yet, ask whether you can be paid after X number of days or on publication, whichever comes first.

■ **Ask for a kill fee.** Make sure that if a publication changes direction before your article is published, you'll at least get a kill fee. Twenty-five percent is standard, but the higher the better. If you get a kill fee, you can walk away with your story and place it elsewhere. (See "If your article gets 'killed,' all you can expect is your kill fee," p. 150.)

■ **Lessen your risk.** You stand less of a chance of getting burned (and any burns will hurt less) if you stick with the familiar and the small. Says freelance writer Kelly James-Enger. "I write [pay-on-pub] for two types of magazines: smaller magazines where I have an ongoing relationship with the editors and write for them every issue, and magazines that purchase reprints to stories." Diana will accept a pay-on-pub contract only if the dollar amount is under $500.

■ **Diversify.** Writing for a few pay-on-pub magazines won't make your financial situation sticky if you can rely on a steady influx of checks from publications that pay on acceptance. "If I started accepting a bunch of magazines that paid on publication all at once, it would be tough," says Cuvelier. "The trick is to have many articles in production at any one time."

Pay-on-pub contracts may not be a boon for writers, but neither are they a bane. Play it smart, negotiate, and don't plan your budget around pay-on-pub assignments – and you can profit from writing for these magazines.

RULE: You should never accept less than $1 per word.

What is it with the magic $1 per word rate? We've had $1 per word assignments where we'd have been better off grinding beans at Starbucks for an afternoon. For example, Linda writes for a magazine that pays a whopping $1.75 per word – but the rate tells only half the story. She once spent a lot of time researching and writing a health article for this magazine. Two weeks later the editor e-mailed to ask Linda to provide prices for all the medical procedures mentioned in the article. So Linda called specialists around the country, many who were reluctant to reveal their fees. A week later, the editor e-mailed again: She wanted Linda to combine two sections. A week after that, the editor sent back the article riddled with more questions that needed to be answered.

The bottom line: With the hourly rate Linda earned on this article, she would have been better off writing for a trade magazine. In fact, at the time, Linda had a regular gig writing project profiles for a technology trade magazine. The pay was only about 25 cents per word, but because it took her only about an hour and a half to do the interview and write each piece, Linda actually earned $160 per hour.

Diana used to write "shorts," 200- to 500-word articles, for *Psychology Today* for the so-so sum of 50 cents per word. However, since her editor would provide story ideas based on recent psychological studies and even provide the source's contact information, all Diana had to do was call or write the source, send questions by e-mail, and summarize the research. It never took more than two hours total to do the work, which meant she was making $100 to $200 per hour. Not bad!

The problem arises when you accept 25-cent-per-word assignments that take days to research and write – and worse, you get an editor who makes you rewrite it a few times. If you sense that this will be the case for you, either negotiate for more money or walk away.

But don't write off lower paying assignments merely because they're not in the magic $1-per-word league: They could boost your cash flow quite nicely if you can write them quickly and get paid quickly. We urge you to think dollars per hour instead of dollars per word.

RULE: If you ask for better contract terms, your editor may take your assignment away.

Get some self-esteem! Besides, do you really want to work for someone who gets hot under the collar about contract changes? Most editors expect negotiation, and may even be surprised if you roll over and play dead with the first terms they give you. Most editors understand what freelancers are up against since many of them freelance on the side, and often they'll work with you, even if only to tell you they're sorry that they can't change the terms, but they'll make sure you're paid quickly. Maybe they'll throw extra money in the pot to sweeten the deal, but you'll never know until you ask.

An editor once called Linda and asked her to write a 2,500-word article for $600. This magazine gave Linda her first assignment several years ago, thereby helping to launch her freelance career, and she continues to write for them out of feelings of nostalgia and obligation. But she figured it was about time she got a raise. All she said was, "Do you think you could raise the pay a little?" and the editor rushed off to ask her editor-in-chief. The editor soon got back on the line with a new offer: $750. Still not great, but it was an extra $150 in Linda's pocket just for asking. And it was so easy, Linda's still kicking herself that she hadn't asked earlier.

Does the idea of negotiating make you want to dive under the covers? Try these tips to up your negotiating power:

■ **Don't say "yes" right away.** If an editor calls to offer a contract, you can get all the details, but you don't have to commit at that moment. Tell the nice editor you'll get back to her in a few hours or the next day, hang up, give your kid a high-five, and then do some quick research with your network.

■ **"That seems a little low to me."** The National Writers Union credits journalist Brett Harvey with coining this phrase, and we've met many other journalists who use it (or a variation thereof) after an editor offers an unsavory rate. It helps if you practice saying it so that you don't sound like a tentative patsy. The other key to using this phrase is to keep your mouth shut — yes, not a word! — after you've put it out there. Even if you experience a few moments of uncomfortable silence, let your editor be the first to respond. There's no need to plead, "My cat has this hairball problem and I need to start buying her an expensive brand of food, so please, please, please pay me more." You can also use this phrase in e-mail negotiations — better, because you don't have to worry about pregnant pauses.

■ **Practice.** Once you've gone through a few of these assignment phone calls (and we hope you get lots of them!) you'll discover that they generally follow the same script. Your editor will talk about the assignment itself — what he expects, what he'd like to see in your finished piece, etc. — and then move to those more mundane matters, like due dates. Diana has found that in some cases she has to *ask* about payment … honest! The editors always sound a bit flustered after Diana asks, "And how much are you offering for this piece?" (Funny, but we think they wouldn't act so discomfited by the mere mention of money if we were negotiating *their* salaries. But we digress.) If you get all muddled about asking for more money or better contract terms, practice with your partner, a friend in your network, or your dog. Or put yourself in the shoes of a master negotiator or someone you really admire. Can you see Bill Gates or Madonna getting wigged out about asking for more money?

RULE: None of the other writers have complained about these terms.

Man, when an editor spews this out on us, we cringe. Not because we're ashamed of ourselves for having the audacity to ask for an extra 25 bucks for electronic rights, but because it's akin to the editor claiming like a six-year-old, "Everyone else is doing it this way, so why can't I?"

If an editor throws this at you during the negotiation phase, you can assure yourself of three things. First, you're probably not the first writer to stand up to him. Second, if you are the first writer to ask him for contract changes, then he probably hasn't been an editor for very long. Third, he's trying to put you on the defensive.

There are a couple of ways to handle this comment and others like it. You can ignore it, pretending it's not out there. Or you can reply, "Hmm, that's interesting." Pause. "Now back to what we were discussing, how does an extra $100 sound?" And if you're feeling so-so about the assignment, you could respond with something cheeky like, "Really? That's funny, because I've never had a problem making this change in other contracts."

Don't let comments like these derail you from your goal. If an editor continues to lob verbal grenades at you during negotiations, it could be his way of intimidating you into accepting the status quo, and maybe you need to rethink how much you really want to work with someone who operates like this. After all, if he's this bullying about a few changes to some legalese, what's he going to be like when he's editing your copy? If you're getting a bad feeling in the pit of your stomach about the editor's interpersonal skills, maybe it's best to take your talents elsewhere. Don't be afraid to walk away.

Chapter

Five

Mining for Information
A Little Digging Can Turn Up Info Gold

If you scramble to find sources for your articles, if you have trouble dealing with PR people, or if you moan over how costly database access is, this chapter is for you. And if these scenarios don't apply to you? Read this chapter anyway. You may find a few new ways to increase the size of your Rolodex.

RULE: You must find original sources.

Sure, original sources are great, but hardly necessary. To find sources, look at other articles similar in subject to yours and take note of who is quoted. You can even go through your own published articles! Why not contact these sources when you're writing an article in roughly the same subject area? When Diana was pitching a story on pet etiquette to a women's magazine, she got quotes from an etiquette consultant she'd profiled for *1099* magazine. When one of Diana's colleagues was looking for a young, hip etiquette expert to interview for an article in *Condé Nast Bride's*, Diana had the perfect source for her.

RULE: Find your own sources; don't ask your editor to help you.

A lot of writers miss a primo timesaving opportunity when they're talking over their article assignments with their editors. They'll ask everything from how long the finished piece should be and when it will run in the magazine to how the editor would like it delivered. But they don't bother to ask, "Is there anyone you know who'd make a great source for this story?"

If you're writing an article for a trade magazine, or on a topic that's near and dear to the general readership of the publication, your editor will often have a Rolodex or PDA crammed with the names of experts, industry analysts he's met at trade shows, or authors who've written seminal books on the subject. Since your editor has his finger on the pulse of his readership, doesn't it make sense to at least ask him?

Often, your editor will happily provide you with several names and appropriate contact information. Voila! Now you don't have to scramble around and spend hours digging for the names yourself. If your editor has spent time thinking about the right people with whom you should speak, often you'll be set for the whole article. This is why writing "shorts" (see "If you write 'shorts' for a magazine, you'll never break in to the 'feature well,'" p. 35) can be so profitable for writers, especially if your editor is calling you with the assignments: Most of the time, you need only one source, and your editor will have this person picked out for you. All you have to do is call or e-mail your hand-picked source.

Sometimes your editor will give you sources that don't pan out. You can always go back to him and ask for more names, or ask the sources you've spoken with if they know anyone else who'd be willing to talk to you.

You should rethink this strategy, however, when you're doing a piece where it's assumed that you're the one who has the edge on appropriate sources. For example, if you're touting yourself as a health and fitness writer to a women's magazine, we think your editor would raise an eyebrow if you asked her for names of appropriate medical experts to interview. Another example would be if you've sold a proposal for a celebrity profile on Colin Firth or a story featuring "people on the street." The editor will naturally assume that you already have access to Mr. Firth (in which case, you should contact Diana now to give her the full scoop), and it's your job to find the "real people" to interview.

RULE: Database access is expensive.

On many of the writer mailing lists we subscribe to, our colleagues like to moan about the high cost of database access. A service like LexisNexis Current Issues, which gives you access to over 8,000 full-text publications, is pricey; last time we checked, it ran $250 a week for access to the newspaper, business, and financial database. However, LexisNexis also has a "pay as you go" service called LexisNexis by Credit Card, where you can do a free search on your subject and pay a small fee only for the legal information, news stories, company and financial information, and public records you download. (See Appendix 5, p. 190.)

Better yet, most freelancers who live in the U.S. can tap into their local public library's EBSCO magazine database from home for free access to thousands of consumer and trade magazines. All it will cost you is one visit to your librarian for a library card, and maybe a stop at the reference desk for instructions.

Most major newspapers around the world have web-based searchable archives that go waaaaay back. If an article has been published recently, sometimes you can read it for free, but if it's older, you may have to pay a small fee for full-text access.

If you have a strong relationship with one of the publications you write for and they happen to have editorial offices nearby, you can ask whether they'll let you tap into their databases. Many publications have subscriptions to LexisNexis, so take advantage of your connections if you have them.

RULE: Your sources must be well-known experts in their fields.

Open up any magazine, and sure, you'll find multitudes of quotes from industry titans, media pundits, celebrities of the moment, and doctors touting eponymous diet books. But look beyond the household names and you'll find just as many expert quotes from people whose names are totally unfamiliar to you.

Your expert sources don't have to be newsprint regulars; in fact, no-name-brand quotes are often better. If you depend on ProfNet to find sources (see Appendix 5, p. 190), it can be embarrassing when your editor informs you that the expert you've quoted in your article pops up in nearly every other article that crosses her desk. (The solution? Do a quick database search on your source to find out whether she's been quoted in the publication in the past. Or, instead of using ProfNet's search query feature, where you get potential sources to contact you, search its database and contact appropriate sources yourself.)

No-name experts often give better quotes because they're not as used to talking to the media. We've spoken with self-proclaimed experts who've spent too much time hanging out with their PR handlers, and their quotes sound like they're on their umpteenth regurgitation. (This proves true most often when speaking with high-level business executives.) It is extremely difficult to get these people to give you a quote that's juicy and fresh and that doesn't sound like it was written by their corporate communications department and vetted by their attorneys.

The key to locating great sources is to not only exploit services like ProfNet, but to mine your everyday life. When Diana landed an assignment about massage anxiety from *Walking*, she did the expected, which was to call the press contact for the American Massage Therapy Association. They put her in contact with several therapists around the country, all of whom were practiced interviewees. But then Diana also interviewed her own massage therapist, a woman who'd never been interviewed before. Diana's masseuse ended up giving her the key quote for her article.

Chapter 5 - Mining for Information

If you're working on a story that features real people and not experts, mine your life. You can start by sending an e-mail to everyone in your address book to let them know what you're working on and what information you need. (Just make sure if you send out a group e-mail that you bcc [blind carbon copy] all of the addresses; give your sources some privacy!). You can also ask everyone you bump into if they know of people who can help you out: your hairdresser, doctor, or therapist, for example, can be goldmines of information.

Since Diana pitches a lot of parenting articles, she pesters everyone in her mothers group and her son's playgroups for potential sources (and story ideas!). She also talks to her son's pediatrician about the best medical experts for certain stories. While working on a pitch about children and chronic back pain, Diana noticed a letter to the editor in her local paper from a parent who was concerned about the weight of his son's backpack. A quick search in the White Pages gave Diana the letter writer's telephone number, so she called him and got great "man on the street" quotes from him for her proposal.

Now you can start moving beyond your neighborhood. Check out Internet newsgroups and web-based bulletin boards. These gathering places can be hostile to journalists, but neither Linda nor Diana have had their hands virtually slapped in cyberspace when they visited such places for the express purpose of finding sources. If you're a frequent, visible visitor to a website or bulletin board, you usually won't have any problem if you post a request for sources. If you don't visit often (or at all), contact the board's administrator and explain your request. Often that little courtesy will get you a warm welcome.

RULE: Public relations people are your friends.

PR agencies and departments answer to their clients, not to you. Sure, they'll act like they're your new best friends, especially if you're writing a cover story for a big newsstand magazine that bathes their client or their client's products in a flattering light. But woe to those writers who depend solely on the kindness of PR departments or agencies when writing for a smaller magazine or about a touchy subject that won't benefit their client.

Here's a cautionary tale: Diana took on a cover story about how staffing agencies account for the high hourly markups on consultant time even though she knew it was going to be difficult to get staffing firms to talk. First of all, the magazine's audience was made up of IT consultants, the people who were purportedly being screwed by these agencies. Second, the agencies would have to explain in detail how they came up with their markup numbers, and they'd have to share this proprietary information not only with consultants, but also with competitors reading the magazine. The agencies gained nothing by speaking with Diana about this subject.

She tracked down sources and plotted a strategy to get staffing firms to talk. Her editor said that as a last resort, Diana could agree with her sources that quotes would not be attributed to them and that their firms would not be identified by name in the story. She also made sure that the PR people knew up front what she was looking for so that there would be no surprises during the interviews.

One associate for a PR firm representing a staffing agency was all over Diana like a fly on honey. Of course the president of the company was willing to talk! He would even call Diana so that the interview wouldn't be on her dime! How nice! Everything was hunky dory, until a few minutes before the scheduled interview when the PR rep called and nervously asked if Diana could forward her the questions for review. With foreboding in her heart, Diana sent an overview of what she was looking for (the same overview she'd sent the flack a week before) and can you guess what *didn't* happen next? The interview. The PR rep sent an e-mail saying that the company president was sorry, but he had to "suddenly" leave his office.

This kind of thing or variations thereof happens (and usually when you've got a tight deadline!), so beware. Many PR professionals, especially those fresh out of college, set up interviews with reporters as if they've got a quota for the month. They'll volunteer their client for anything ("My client, the leading provider of e-mail filtering software, is the perfect source for your article on new developments in dandruff control!"), but when the client is apprised of the topic, he backs out of the interview – and rightfully so. We've done far too many interviews where the interviewee is at a complete loss as to why he's talking to us. It's a total waste of his time, as well as ours, and we're not polite to the PR rep afterwards.

Once you start working on lots of assignments, you'll need to manage your PR contacts. We suggest that you get several free e-mail accounts. This will allow you to give PR contacts an alternative e-mail address so you won't have to sift through tons of boring press releases to read your regular e-mail. Diana has the ability to create as many e-mail addresses as she wants with her web domain name. When she posts a query at ProfNet, for example, she creates a new address that's relevant to the story she's currently working on – a story on kids and pet allergies, for example, might have an address such as allerpetpress@ninetofive.com. Occasionally, a PR firm will start bombarding her with press releases months later; by checking the e-mail address they've used, Diana can tell whether they're using her address improperly. When this happens, she reports them to ProfNet and they get their wrists slapped for abusing writers' e-mail addresses.

RULE: PR people are your enemies.

Based on our last rule breaker, you're probably thinking that we don't have a whit of respect for the PR profession. Wrong! Yes, a few flakes and kooks exist, but let's be fair: PR reps can match our horror stories with tales of freelance writers who have flaked and kooked out on them. The bottom line is that at some point in your freelancing career, you'll have to go through a PR agency or rep to get to your source, and you need to learn how to work with these generally affable folks. Don't forget that you need them as much as they need you.

Now, Diana has a unique perspective on the writer/agency/ source relationship, because she used to be the person that journalists scrambled to reach when they needed a quote for breaking news in the household adhesives market. Whenever the media called her company, they were forwarded to an account executive at her company's retained public relations firm for screening.

PR agencies are looking to get their clients the best possible coverage, so if a writer representing a big-name publication like *Better Homes & Gardens* or *This Old House* approached the agency, they would be whisked to the interview table. Reporters from key trade publications also got this kind of snap-to-it service. But after that, there was a definite pecking order as to which journalists got through and which ones didn't. A feature writer from a small newspaper chain in northern Minnesota would not get this kind of attention, and a freelancer who didn't have a firm assignment from a publication would get even less. Usually, the PR agency would simply send a press kit to these folks, or give them quotes as the company's official representatives.

So, if you've got a firm assignment from a major publication, you'll probably have no trouble getting PR reps to take your calls and set up appointments with their ivory-towered clients. But what if you fall in that second or third tier of writers? If you really need to get through to a key source, and you feel that the PR agency is going to run interference, how can you get them to listen to you?

The key is to position your request so that it's in the PR agency's best interest to help you. Don't expect them to figure this out on their own, or you'll soon find yourself holding one of their client's press kits filled with boring, corporate-speak copy. Let's make up an example: You're pitching a story to a parenting magazine about whether or not babies benefit from all the videotapes that are marketed to their overachieving parents. You'd love to quote the founder of a top educational toy company, but she's guarded by overprotective flacks. In your request to her company's PR department, be honest – don't lie and tell them you have the assignment. We know a few writers who've done this, only to have it backfire when the suspicious PR rep called the magazine to confirm the assignment. How embarrassing! But if parenting and education are your beats, make sure they know that, and tell them what other magazines you've worked with. If you don't do this, you're losing a great opportunity to convince them that it's in their future best interests to set up this interview for you, even if this interview doesn't guarantee press for their client. If you don't have this kind of ammo, then put the best possible spin on your request. How many people will be reading your article? If the founder doesn't speak with you, will it make her look bad?

Once you have their attention, make sure they know what you need from their client. Often, PR reps will ask you for the questions ahead of time: They'll say their client needs them to prepare. Ninety-nine percent of the time, we'll oblige (see "Don't send your questions to the source," p. 112). If you think that not providing the questions will be a deal-breaker and you really need this interview, go ahead and do so, keeping in mind that you're certainly free to ask any question you like during the actual interview. What we like to do is provide the PR reps with an overview of what we're looking for, and that usually helps them prepare their client.

When you're dealing with a PR agency, it's a good bet that they've done a lot of work to set up the interview for you, especially if the person you're speaking with is a high-level executive, so make sure you call when you're supposed to, not five minutes later. Often, the agency will call you, which is great, because it saves on your phone bill, especially if you've got a talkative source. When this happens, your source is usually patched in to the call with the PR agency listening in on the interview. Some agencies will insist on listening in, usually so they can later coach their client on how to answer any questions he flubbed. If you want to fight that, that's your call. Diana doesn't mind the eavesdropping – she always tells agency reps up front that if they say anything, she won't quote them, so she usually hears them filing their nails in the background as she conducts the interview.

It's not difficult to develop a snarling attitude toward public relations professionals, because when they screw a writer over, they usually screw them memorably. So when we meet a PR person who has done a great job setting up interviews, providing helpful information, and prepping his client for a productive interview, we go out of our way to thank him and make him feel appreciated.

RULE: You have to go through the PR agency/department.

Many journalists automatically search for the telephone number of the PR department to make initial contact with a source. Reconsider this. Why? Because the PR department, not your source, will decide whether or not your interview is worthy of the source's time. At best, the PR department can take a few days to get back to you ... bad news if you're under a tight deadline. At worst, your request gets buried under all the other requests they're fielding, especially if it's a company or organization that attracts a lot of publicity.

If you have the name of the person you want to talk to, skip the PR people and call or e-mail her directly with your request. Sometimes she'll give you the information you need right on the phone. Other times she'll tell you she can't talk until she clears it with her superiors. Even then, that's better than relying on a third-party to set up initial contact.

Recently, Diana interviewed some extremely busy magazine editors for an article. She did a little research, found a few editors who could speak knowledgeably on the topic, then contacted them directly. One editor simply asked for the questions and answered them by e-mail. The second editor needed to clear things with her boss first, but approval to speak came within a day. The third answered Diana's questions, and actually gave the questions to her boss to answer, too! Had Diana gone through the appropriate PR channels, she believes she'd still be waiting for the seas to part, the heavens to open, and the angels to belt out "Hallelujah." The worst that can happen is that your source will insist you go through her PR department or agency, but even then, you'll have more leverage when you approach these PR people with a warmed-up source on your side.

RULE: You can never have too many sources or too much research for a story.

Ah, the classic rationalization of an inveterate procrastinator. Going to the library, surfing the Web, e-mailing potential sources – all these things sound productive, and they are … to a certain point.

We find that we start believing this bad ol' rule when we're writing for a new editor or publication, and we want to impress them with our reporting skills. We'll spend hours searching the Web for one more statistic, one more factoid that will make our article sparkle and gleam. We also fall into this trap when we're tackling a subject we've never covered before or a lengthy assignment where we have more leeway on content.

With long, fact-intensive pieces, Diana stops doing "research" when she notices that her sources start sounding alike, and the new quotes and information she's getting parrots what she's already researched. She also keeps the length of her article in mind when she's looking for sources – a 200-word short requires only one source, while a 2,000-word technology story may require five or six sources. One good rule of thumb is to interview one person for every 500 words, plus one more for good measure. So a 500-word article will have two sources, and a 1,500-word piece will have four.

RULE: Don't trust the Web.

Back when writers took their first steps onto the Information Highway, this rule was practically hammered into their heads. This rule made plenty of sense, then – there was (and yes, there still is) a lot of crap that gets posted and taken for gospel. But we do believe that the quality of information you can find on the World Wide Web has improved dramatically. Check out sites like dictionary.com, which help you check the spelling of the word, or The Smoking Gun (www.thesmokinggun.com), a fun and informative site that takes advantage of the Freedom of Information Act to let you read Winona Ryder's probation reports and autopsy results of the rich and famous.

We think the Web has made the lives of freelancers a heck of a lot easier, and it should get the credit it deserves. As long as you double-check the information you find, don't treat what you read as gospel, and stick with reputable sites, you should be fine – in short, be a good reporter.

What kinds of sites will give you a good start on research?

■ **Google (www.google.com).** What would we do if we couldn't Google? This is the best search engine on the Web because it indexes more web pages and returns more relevant results than other engines.

■ **Federal, state, and local governments.** You can find which U.S. city has the highest number of violent crimes in a certain year, download economic reports, or check out the State Department's warnings about foreign travel.

■ **Colleges and universities.** Larger universities have on-line access to library holdings, directories of phone numbers for their top experts, and research studies to peruse.

■ **Major corporations.** If you're looking for financial information about a publicly held company, the SEC is monitoring them, so the information you find should be accurate – Enron and WorldCom excepted.

■ **Major media, print and broadcast.** Places like *The New York Times*, *The Wall Street Journal*, *BBCNews.com*, and *CNN.com*.

Chapter **Six**

Talking the Talk
Renegade Interviews Get the Story, and Then Some

Here are the rules: First you have to rack your brain formulating the perfect interview questions, then you have to wrangle good quotes out of your source, and then you have to spend hours transcribing your interview tapes. Yeah, right – if that were true, Diana and Linda would have quit long ago. Read on for the secrets to getting the most out of your interviews without going bonkers in the process.

RULES: Write up your questions ahead of time and stick to them.

Having a list of questions that you need answered during an interview is a good idea, but remember that your questions are more like the signposts along the journey, not the road map. Sometimes you can get so wedded to your list that you don't bother to listen to what your source is telling you; you're in a hurry to move on to the next question. Other times the interviewee doesn't understand something you've asked, and you let the question slide, figuring that you'll come back to it later. Most importantly, sticking rigidly to your list prevents you from asking better questions that may come up during your interview – answers to which may give your article more juice.

If you get queasy during interviews (like Linda) or you're a new freelancer, a prepared list of questions can reduce anxiety, especially if you know what information you specifically need from a source. Diana, for example, runs through the same basic questions for all of her interviews – she asks the person to spell his name and give his proper job title, and she double-checks contact information. She created a checklist to make sure she gets this info right away. If certain facts must be confirmed by the source, she'll write those down, too. Once those are out of the way, she asks an overview question about the subject that naturally leads to the next question and so on. When she listens to the tape later, the interview sounds like a relaxed conversation, not a segment on "Firing Line."

RULE: Don't send your questions to the source ahead of time.

Some writers think if you send your questions to the source ahead of time, you'll hear nothing but rehearsed, canned responses. But this has never been the case in Linda's experience. Sending a list of questions lets the source prepare for the interview and ensures that you'll get well-thought-out answers. Linda doesn't send every question she might possibly ask, but simply compiles an overview list of the topics she'd like to cover. For example, while working on an article on food-borne illnesses for *Oxygen*, Linda sent the following list of questions to her sources:

1. Which foods have been the worst culprits in spreading food-borne illnesses?

2. How do foods get infected on the field, during processing, at the market, and in the home?

3. Is the situation in the U.S. getting better or worse?

4. What's being done by the government to protect con-

sumers against food-borne illnesses?

5. What can consumers do to protect themselves?

Of course, this is a huge topic and Linda could have asked dozens of other questions – but these were the most important for her article, and they were enough to give the sources an idea of what she was looking for. During the actual interviews, Linda asked additional questions targeted to her sources' areas of expertise.

If you're doing an investigative story, sending questions ahead of time may be tricky, especially if you have a wily source. In that case, you can provide her with an overview of what you'll be talking about, and sometimes that will be enough to please her.

RULE: Formulate your own interview questions.

Many freelance writers carry this crazy notion in their head that they have to do everything for themselves: find their sources, figure out what questions to ask, and then conduct the interview. Why not do what one writer we know does? When he's discussing an assignment over the phone with his editor, he'll ask, "What questions do *you* want answered in this article?" Usually, his editor will come up a handful of great questions, which the writer then asks his sources.

If you're profiling someone, whether she's famous or unknown beyond her industry, ask a friend, family member, or colleague, "What would you like to know about this person?" The same question can be retooled for a travel article ("What would you want to know if you were planning a bike trip to Nova Scotia?") or even a service piece ("What would you consider a huge etiquette faux pas in the workplace?").

Another trick is to ask your source at the end of an interview, "Is there a question that you thought I would ask but haven't?" Often, you'll get some interesting responses to this. One of Diana's cheekier sources answered, "Yeah, I thought you were going to ask me out." Guess he didn't hear Diana's husband puttering around in the office next door.

RULE: Face-to-face interviews take up too much valuable time.

When Diana was a feature writer for a local chain of papers (and sort of new to the whole freelancing game), she met nearly every one of her sources in person to interview them. Most of the time the interviews stuck to the time Diana allotted for them and she got great visual details that added to her stories. For example, she was interviewing the director of a local weight loss clinic when a couple came in for their weekly appointment. The couple agreed to share their story, and luckily, the newspaper's photographer arrived in time to capture their weigh-in.

Diana knows a more experienced writer who pooh-poohs face-to-face meetings because they "gobble up too much time." This writer insists on telephone or e-mail interviews, period. True, some interviews can be handled this way, but other stories require a more personal touch. Pick up any newsstand magazine and figure out which writer interviewed the celebrity in person and which writer interviewed the celebrity over the phone. Sometimes the writer has no choice, especially when he's working with celebrities and their attendant handlers. But stories that describe how a starlet hid her bloodshot eyes behind dark RayBans during a lunch interview at an LA hotspot are more interesting than ones that merely report what the starlet said about her latest movie. And if you're interested in literary journalism, do you think for a moment that John McPhee interviewed geologists and orange farmers from the comfort of his home office? Or that Sebastian Junger didn't hang out in Gloucester, Massachusetts, to absorb the feel of the fishing community he was writing about? They probably had nice expense accounts, but still – if this is the kind of writing you want to do, you need to get out there and get your hands dirty.

Most of our interviews are conducted by telephone or e-mail

because that's what our stories require. If you're writing a service article for *Woman's Day* on how to clean a house in an hour, it makes little sense to meet your experts and sources in person. But an in-depth profile of a local company with an innovative product? We'd go for the face-to-face time. Think about what your story requires to be the best that it can be, and forget the rules that keep you tethered to your telephone.

RULE: Transcribing interview tapes takes hours.

We usually tape our interviews, but we learned early on that if you're working on several meaty assignments at once, transcribing tapes gobbles up precious time. You should ask yourself whether the interview is important enough to have on tape, and if it is, whether you need to have every word in hard copy. In certain cases we feel it's worth having a complete interview transcript, such as when we're speaking to someone about a controversial subject or the interviewee is giving us complex and vital information that may confuse us if we only take notes. Other times, we tape and make notes while we're talking, then go back and transcribe only the important parts of the interview. After all, no law says the whole tape has to be transcribed. However, there are very strict laws about taping phone calls, so check your state's laws and guidelines before you go crazy with your recorder. (One thing we never do is tape over interviews – tape is cheap, but lawsuits are not. Buy tapes in bulk and store your taped interviews somewhere where the dog won't chew them up.)

Which brings us to a clause that lawyers like to sneak into contracts: "All notes, tapes, materials and transcripts must be turned over to the publisher." Linda and Diana have never had an editor request these materials, and if they did, we'd be loath to turn them over. We've talked to a lot of writers, and they agree with us – unless the magazine is paying for your transcription services, the transcripts are yours, not theirs. So strike this clause if you see it, and if they won't, give them a price for this service.

If you decide you want a full transcript but don't have the

time, then do what we do – talk someone else into doing it for you by dangling cold, hard cash in front of them. Linda once hired a college student to transcribe her tapes when she was too busy to do it herself. She paid the student $30 per tape, and most of her articles had only one to one-and-a-half tapes worth of interviews. It was well worth the $30 to $45 to avoid the hassle of transcribing the tapes, especially since the articles paid from $400 to $2,500.

Diana interviewed a couple of local professional transcriptionists and hired the best of the lot to transcribe hours of interviews she needed for a consuming investigative feature. Once she delegated this task, a burden left her shoulders and she felt energized to work on other parts of the project. Was it worth the cost? Absolutely, when you consider she then freed up her time to do the things she's good at doing, like finding more work.

But when it comes to hiring a transcriptionist, caveat emptor. Linda once used a transcription agency that specialized in medicine and law. They charged more than 100 smackers to transcribe the interviews for one article, and the results were astoundingly bad. The transcriptionist consistently wrote "e-commerce" as "e-comma" – who in the universe hadn't heard of e-commerce by the year 2001? Also, whenever a word had a homonym, she would invariably pick the wrong one: "website" became "Web sight," "too" became "two." Finally, the transcription was riddled with notes saying that particular sections were "unintelligible" – and when Linda went back to listen to those parts, they were perfectly audible.

So how do you find a good transcriptionist? Diana used the Yellow Pages and sought out the lowest price and quickest turnaround, which worked out for her because the interviews weren't very technical. To find her college student helper, who did a great job, Linda posted a request on the online bulletin boards of local colleges. Places like MediaBistro.com and the subscription-based sites like Freelance Success and The Well (see Appendix 12, p. 196) can also put you in touch with someone who's willing to transcribe during a slow time in his schedule. Sometimes a writer with no assignments on his plate will take on such work, and he'll probably be a pretty accurate transcriptionist.

If you're a crack typist, however, you can do what Eric does: He types his interviewees' answers right into his computer during the interview. He captures about 75 percent of the conversation, making sure he gets all the important information and leaving out repetitions, asides, and so on. He makes up abbreviations on the fly, and goes back to fill in missing information once the interview ends. There's even software that will automatically expand any abbreviation you define.

Diana, who's a decent typist, can't concentrate on typing and talking at the same time, so she's looking into buying a digital pen, which has a sensor that captures your writing movements. When you're done, you can download the pen's contents into your computer – no retyping!

RULE: People love to talk about themselves.

This may be true at dinner parties, but it's often not the case when you've cornered an interview subject and begin firing away, especially if he's shown any reluctance to speak with you. Getting great quotes even from "hot" sources can be difficult, but getting them from someone who's lukewarm takes a tremendous amount of skill, patience, and often outright cunning.

Once, for a job trend story for an IT magazine, one of Diana's regular sources put her in contact with a software programmer he talked up as "the dream job candidate," someone who'd be perfect to interview for this story. This programmer was brilliant, tops in his field, and the recruiter was sure this guy would have great stories to share about his work life.

This source may have been a "dream job candidate," but he was a limp noodle on audiotape. For starters, he had a thick accent that was hard to understand. Diana's attempts to warm him up with her brief comedy routine at the beginning of the interview were greeted with silence. While sweat trickled down Diana's back, the programmer figured out how to answer every one of her open-ended questions with a monotone "Yes" or "No."

Afterwards, Diana reviewed her notes and listened to the monologue on her tape recorder, and found not a single good quote to use in this story. Nothing. Zilch. So she e-mailed the programmer a couple of "I just need some clarification" questions. This time, he added a few new answers to his standard retinue of "Yes" and "No": some compelling "Maybes" and gripping "I don't knows." Still not one quote to be found. She reclaimed the interview by writing about the source in the third-person, and then asking a job recruiter to comment on this programmer's skill set.

Interviewing someone who's tongue-tied can drive a writer to panic, but the little tricks below can improve or salvage the experience.

■ **Perfect your lead-in.** Many times you're so eager to bag your prey that you forget to lure them into your camp. It's important to spend a little time courting your source because then you can assess whether you'll need two pens to keep up with him, or you'll need to whip out advanced tricks to get him to talk. Your lead-in can be businesslike ("Thanks for speaking with me today, John. I need your expertise for this article I'm writing for *Business Monthly* about credit card fraud.") or frightfully mundane ("So, how are the Santa Ana winds treating you this year?"). Think of it as dinner party chitchat, but you only have to do it for a minute.

■ **Tell them what you want.** No, we're not advising you to make up quotes and attribute them to your tight-lipped sources. But it helps to remember that your interviewee usually isn't privy to the big picture of your story. If you can explain how she fits into your piece ("I need a few quotes from a security expert about how homeowners can protect their valuables"), this may be enough to relax her. When Diana worked as a marketing communications manager for a packaged goods company, reporters from trade publications often contacted her to talk about her industry's packaging issues. It was disconcerting when a reporter called and peppered her with questions without explaining the piece he was working on. Was it an exposé on the shady tactics marketers use to sell products? Or was it a roundup about the challenges marketers face when they sell their products overseas?

■ **Get it in writing.** Certain people do much better with e-mail interviews. People who choke up on the phone are often great quotesmiths on paper (like writers, for example). E-mail interviews are also attractive to sources because they can answer the questions at their leisure and take the time to come up with the perfect replies. You can ask, "Would you be more comfortable writing out your answers, or should I call you?" To save time during a busy month, Linda once wrote an entire article using nothing but e-mail interviews. It turned out great! The only problem with e-mail interviews is that you miss the opportunity for on-the-fly follow-up questions.

■ **Forget the word "interview."** Refer to the interrogation as a "conversation," a "talk," or a "chat" – anything *but* an interview – and that may be enough to thaw a nervous source. In fact, if this is a really important interview for you, try to spend as much time with your source as you can doing anything *but* interviewing. Then, when she's relaxed, ask her a few easy questions. Then go back to the chitchat. You'll notice that some of the well-known network interviewers do this: Diane Sawyer often looks like she's best friends with her subject, until she moves closer and asks her, "Now, Sue, tell me … did you murder your husband?"

■ **Feel their pain.** Share a little. When Diana interviewed women who had been dealing with physically and emotionally painful fertility problems for a potential story, she let them know that she, too, had run the medical gantlet of reproductive issues. It helped these women to know they were speaking with someone who understood what they were going through.

■ **When all else fails, tell them *exactly* what you want.** If you're paying attention, you'll notice that we mentioned something like this a couple of bullet points ago. Only now we add the word *exactly*. When you've got a source who simply can't give good quote, you need to help him out. Think of what you would like him to say, and then start this out with "Would you agree that …" or "Is it accurate to say …." Your source's words can be salvaged by writing "Jones *agrees* that Dr. Smith's latest diet book is filled with nutritional misinformation." Or the opposite if he doesn't agree. You don't actually have to quote him, unless your editor is adamant about having copy between quotation marks.

RULE: Don't let the interview veer off course.

One of the most rewarding aspects of a freelance writing career is getting to talk to interesting people. Sure, a lot of times your interviews are rote, but now and then you'll find someone who gives you a katrillion ideas for new stories. If you're married to a list of questions or have set a strict time limit for the interview, it can be very frustrating. That's why flexibility is important. Here's an example:

Diana was looking for a local business that used offshore software programmers on IT projects, so she sent an e-mail to her source network for help. One of her contacts happened to have read a newspaper article about a business like this, so she sent Diana the company name. Diana called and explained to the business owner what she was looking for, and the man invited her to his office since it was in the next town over.

It was one of the most profitable hours Diana has ever spent with a source. Although the article's focus was not going to put this guy's business in the best light with her target audience (American information technology workers who were losing jobs to offshore workers), her source was still willing to share his controversial point of view with these readers.

What was more interesting was that this guy was from China, and he was pursuing the American dream with glee. His enthusiasm for his business was infectious. He had created unique software tools to enable his employees in China to work closely with clients in the U.S. He had just become a U.S. citizen and was proud of what he had achieved in his adopted country.

Over the next several months, Diana came back to this interview to sell more stories. A sister publication of the one she originally wrote for wanted a cover story on the overseas software development market. Her source had given her an excellent overview, so she added another $2,500 to her pocket. Ka-ching! Then she pitched and sold a story to a website about how companies with offices in different time zones improve communications. Ka-ching! A trade magazine, *eCommerce Business*, assigned a piece on web-based offshore software development. Ka-ching! another $2,000 to the coffers. Diana was nowhere near exhausting the well of information this source opened up for her. In less than six months she'd earned over $6,000 from this one interview.

Freelancer Bethanne Kelly Patrick also lets her interviews "flow" and often turns up interesting new angles to her stories, or new stories altogether. For example, one day she was talking to a publishing executive about new book titles, and he mentioned author Carl Hiaasen. She happened to be a Hiaasen fan, and their conversation led Patrick to write a short piece about the quirky author's friendship with musician Warren Zevon.

So don't be afraid to let the interview wander off course, and train your ear for information that might give your article a different spin, or perhaps even spur a proposal for a totally different story. If the interview is interesting and you both have time to spare, feel free to let the conversation take on a life of its own. You never know where it will lead you.

RULE: It's impolite to interrupt.

Ah, yes. The runaway interview. Where your source is rambling on and on about his great grandmother Billings – or was it his great grandmother Michaels? – whose pole beans won not one, not two, but three blue ribbons at the Iowa State Fair. And before you can interject a question that brings the interview back on track, he's off and running about how you should write an article on the inequities of State Fair judging. It's all fixed these days, you know. And he proceeds to tell you why, starting with the 1960 fair he attended when he was 10, and did he tell you how he ate twelve corndogs in one sitting? The best damn corndogs he's ever had because they were made with ....

We've been there. We feel your pain. We've suffered through too many of these interviews and we've learned that in these cases, damn the etiquette books – it's okay to cut these talkative folks off at the first utterance of "May I digress?" No, they may not and yes, we're advising *interviewus interruptus*. Sure, we said above that you should be open to letting the interview veer off course, but only you can tell whether that off-course rambling will net you more ideas – or simply waste your energy.

If it's the latter, do we even need to point out what a huge waste of time and money this is for you? If you're taping and transcribing the interview, you're going to have to listen to this person drone on yet again just to get the interesting bits you managed to wrangle from his flapping lips. (And if you've been listening to *our* flapping lips to this point, you're now paying someone to do your transcriptions. You'll be doubly annoyed when you receive twelve pages of this bigmouth's blathering and a big fat transcription bill for the pleasure.)

There's something else to consider if you're shy about dealing with a motormouth: what happens after the article appears. In our many, many years of experience (ha!) we've discovered that these loquacious sources are not shy about picking up the phone to complain about the scanty coverage you gave them in your article after they spent so long talking with you. That means another time-wasting intervention with this annoying person. Do you want to listen to him all over again, only this time with a serious attitude problem?

Nip it in the bud. If you're new to freelancing, and you've done only a few interviews in your short career, it won't be long before you get one of these windbags on the phone and realize, "Hey, I think this is who the Renegade Writers were talking about. This guy's generating more wind than a church bean supper." You'll know you've butted heads with a runaway interviewee when she doesn't need to take a breath between sentences and says things like, "Before I answer that question, let me first tell you about my (select one) company's business philosophy / Marie Osmond doll collection / complete medical history." If you're not so fresh on the freelancing scene, you've probably developed a sixth sense about interviewing and know within seconds that your source is a wind-up motormouth.

Diana has found that a bit of interview prep helps cut down on mouth froth. First, she usually tells her interviewees prior to the interview what questions she needs answered so they arrive at the conversation with a goal in mind (see "Don't send your questions to the source ahead of time," p. 112). Another trick she learned from her job as a marketing manager is to set a time limit for the interview. You can do this two ways: you can hammer it into your source a couple of times that this a ten-, 15-, or 30-minute interview, or you can fib a bit and tell them you have another appointment that follows. This may feel like a Big Fat Lie to you, but is it really? Does your source need to know that your next appointment is with a grilled cheese sandwich, tomato soup, and Dr. Phil?

Speaking of honesty, a bit of that can help, especially when sprinkled with a liberal amount of flattery. Diana often tells her more verbose interviewees that as much as she'd love to chat all afternoon because they're so interesting (the flattery), this assignment has a word limit (the truth) and she doesn't want to waste their valuable time (more flattery) just to get one itty bitty quote (more honesty). This usually brings interviewees back to planet Earth.

RULE: Give your interviewees a verbal 'thanks.'

Of course you should thank your sources when you're winding up the interview – but that's not all you should do. Many writers send written thank-yous to their sources. It takes only a minute to jot down a quick note, and written thank-you notes from a writer are so rare that sources will definitely remember you kindly when you need to interrupt their busy schedules again in the future.

Linda buys nice, simple thank you cards in bulk from the local discount store. Whenever she finishes an article, she grabs a card and writes: "Thank you for participating in my article on how to crack a coconut for *Marooned Monthly*! Your comments are sure to be very helpful to readers." She then tosses in a business card and drops it in the mail. Diana, on the other hand, pulls out her best Crane notecards and uses them to jot a personal thanks to her sources.

And for sources who go above and beyond the call of duty to help you with an article, a small gift may be in order. Linda has a source she calls again and again for nutrition articles. When this nutritionist spent several hours of her vacation putting together a six-day sugar-free diet, Linda was so grateful that she sent her a basket of handmade soaps.

This isn't to say that you should ever pay or bribe sources. If a source asks to be compensated for his time, head the other way. Paying sources brings up an ethical dilemma: You want an unbiased opinion, but a source who's being paid is likely to tell you only what you want to hear. We also don't accept gifts from our sources, although we know of many ethical, conscientious colleagues who will accept a box of Belgian chocolates around the holidays. We just think there's no harm in sending a small, inexpensive token of thanks to sources who regularly share their expertise with you.

RULE: You have to do your own interviews.

During a period when Linda had more assignments than she had time, she hired another writer to conduct interviews for her. Linda would find the source and write up the questions, and the other writer would set and conduct the interview and send Linda the transcript. Even after six years of freelancing, Linda hates doing interviews and is simply not that good at them, and the writer she hired was an excellent interviewer.

If you're overloaded with work and think you'd like to hire someone to handle your interviews, your best bet may be to hire a magazine or newspaper writer who's looking to make a few extra bucks. You can find likely candidates by keeping an eye on online forums and e-mail discussion groups that cater to writers (see Appendix 12, p. 196).

Chapter / Seven

Putting Pen to Paper
Yes, Renegade Writers Even Break Grammar Rules!

The grammar rules we break in this chapter would make your eighth-grade English teacher faint. And if that isn't incentive enough to read this chapter, we also tell you how to write about your sex life without your mother finding out, how to get free fact-checking for your articles, and when it can be okay to miss your deadline.

RULE: Don't procrastinate; write your article well before your deadline.

It's a simple fact that many of us work better with a little fire burning under our butts. Our advice is to work within your own comfort level. Diana and Linda research and interview weeks before deadline, but save the actual writing until a few days before D-day. Writer Monique Cuvelier has interviewed for and written 3,000-word articles on the day they're due, and she does a damn good job of it, too. That's because at her previous job as a newspaper writer she perfected her super-sleuthing skills and learned to write tight and fast.

There's no need to beat the deadline by weeks or even by days – your editor likely won't even look at the article until after the deadline anyway. However, you may want to give yourself at least a few days to write the article. That way you can put the article aside for a day or so and examine it with a fresh eye while doing the final edit. You can catch a lot of bloopers that way.

When Linda was starting out, she always gave herself three days to write an article once she finished the research. On day one, she wrote half the article. On day two, she wrote the second half. And on day three, she printed it out and went over the whole thing with a red pen, repeating this process several times until she was happy with the piece. She then had Eric give the article a going-over. The day before the deadline, Linda printed it out one final time and checked it for overlooked mistakes before turning it in.

Now that she has more experience, Linda has streamlined the process – not printing out the article so many times, for example, and not running it by her husband (unless she's having trouble with the piece) – but she still gives herself two days to write it, and she turns it in the day before the deadline whenever possible.

RULE: If an editor gives you an assignment topic, that means it's a good story.

Sometimes it seems that editors sit behind their desks brainstorming the most preposterous, undoable ideas, fob them off on their writers, and then trot down to Starbucks for a Frappuccino while the writer runs in circles trying to research The Impossible Article.

An idea that sounds good on paper doesn't always work out in real life. Almost every writer has a horror story about the article topic that wouldn't behave.

Once, the editor of a utilities trade mag asked Linda to find industry analysts who would compare and grade different types of online billing systems. Sounds great, but a couple of problems arose. First of all, none of the analysts – some of whom represented the systems to be compared – wanted to stick their necks out by grading products. Second, the billing systems came in so many different formats that comparisons were meaningless, which the analysts repeatedly told Linda.

Linda contacted the editor three weeks before the deadline to let him know the topic wasn't working. The editor suggested she contact more analysts. She did that, and two weeks before the deadline, Linda called the editor to tell him the topic *still* wasn't working – the new analysts wouldn't talk, either, and they insisted that comparing these products made no sense. Again, the editor suggested she speak to more analysts. Desperate, Linda wrote to several writers' e-mail discussion lists she belonged to, begging for help. The writers sympathized, but had no solutions.

The deadline came, as deadlines are wont to do, and Linda still had no article. The editor was furious; it turns out that the deadline came on his last day on the job, and now he would have to spend extra time there to write the article himself. No wonder he kept urging Linda to keep at it! Linda never got another assignment from that magazine, and as far as she knows, the article topic never appeared.

Sometimes a change in slant will solve the problem of the impossible article. In one instance, Linda was assigned an article on how small business owners can follow their business plan. Hundreds of books are dedicated to this topic, but the editor wanted it in 1,500 words. Good luck. Linda spoke with a few experts and discovered a common theme: A business plan is always a work in progress, and sometimes it shouldn't be followed. With the editor's permission, Linda then wrote the article about how and when to change your plan.

So, if you feel that a story is not working out, let your editor know as soon as possible. Most editors will be willing to slant the idea differently, or even give you another idea that's more doable.

RULE: Never mess with a quote.

When we asked several editors and successful writers if they'd feel comfortable cleaning up their sources' quotes, we almost started a writer's war, complete with lobbed fountain pens and zinging paperclips. You'd have thunk we asked them about cleaning up their sources' bathrooms.

"No. It is not [acceptable to change a quote]," says writer Judy Waytiuk. "If the quote needs cleaning up, keep the part that works, paraphrase the rest – accurately – and put in quotes only the direct quote material you've actually used."

That's the ideal, but it's an ideal that writers find hard to live up to. "I've tried to be good and quote 100 percent. But there's a problem with this because normal speech doesn't lend itself to written text very well," says writer Maggie Bonham. "What you end up doing is making your source look like an idiot. What's better is to put the quote in coherent sentences and not change the context. Make them look smart and like experts and you'll never get a complaint." Bonham may have something there, judging by how many sources have asked Linda and Diana to "clean up the quotes" and not make them "sound stupid."

Elisa Bosley, senior food editor of *Delicious Living* admits she tinkers. "I often change quotes slightly to get them to flow better or make grammatical sense," she says. "People rarely talk in neat, printable quotes. Just don't change the meaning in any way, and verify [the quote] with the person."

It's safe to remove the "um"s and "er"s and you'll probably get your source's undying gratitude if you clean up their grammar. If you want to make changes beyond that, paraphrase the ideas instead of using direct quotes. For example, instead of writing, "'Er, I don't like me that there, um, Atkins diet,' says Donna Danglingparticiple, RD," try, "Donna Danglingparticiple, RD, doesn't like the Atkins diet."

However, in certain cases you do want to capture the unique speech patterns, the hesitancies, and the mangled grammar of your sources. Say you're writing a story on the sharp decline of student test scores in a school district, and your sources are pointing fingers at the new educational consultant who was hired around the time scores started to plummet. When you interview her, you find that she can barely get a sentence out of her mouth without committing a humorous malapropism. In this case, would you clean up the quote? She'd probably be happy if she discovered you'd changed "indecent" to "indigent" for her, but using her exact words would have more impact with the "indecent families" of her district.

RULE: Don't write anything you wouldn't want your mother to see.

All too often our assignments – or our artistic sensibilities – require us to expose our foibles, rehash humiliating anecdotes about our friends and family, or reveal intimate details about our sex lives. How can we deal with the dilemma of writing for an audience of thousands on topics we wouldn't mention to our own mothers? How does a writer write about, say, his search for the perfect toupée, knowing that his friends and family will soon be privy to his hair-raising secret?

■ **Lie like a rug.** Linda subscribes to this technique herself. When her mother-in-law asked her what articles she was working on, no way was Linda about to tell her that she had finished a saucy article for *Redbook* called "The Better Orgasm Diet"; instead, she said that she had written a piece on "nutrition." (Of course, now her mother-in-law knows the truth!)

Greg Blanchette is another writer who uses this approach. Blanchette undertook an ambitious sailing voyage around the world in a small, open boat, and wrote a series of articles about the trip for a sailing magazine. "My parents, of course, wanted copies of the articles," says Blanchette. "What makes a good article in a sailing mag is thrills, danger, narrow escapes – of which there were plenty. But that's not what a parent wants to read. So I assured them that the hairy parts were played up for dramatic effect. They weren't."

■ **Protect the innocent.** You're reading an article about people with a shoe-sniffing fetish, and you notice that one of the names is marked with an asterisk. Your gaze drops to the bottom of the page, where it notes, "This name has been changed." Is your enjoyment of the article any less now that you know the fetishist's name has been changed? Of course not.

Before you try this tactic, check with your editor. *Redbook* was once interested in a slightly raunchy idea of Linda's, but their new policy required sources to use their real names. The result: Although Linda found plenty of anonymous anecdotes, she couldn't scrounge up a single person who wanted to talk about their bedroom romps on the record.

■ **Fake your name.** By day, Jane Simons* writes service pieces for family magazines. By night, she becomes Felicity West, a risqué writer who pens erotica for a living. Pen names are yet another tool for the wallflower writer. "My erotica writing might prove both embarrassing to my family and detrimental to my other writing projects, especially for the family magazines," says Simons. "Using a pen name allows me to write erotica, which pays fairly well, without compromising the rest of my assignments. It's not that I'm ashamed of what I write; it's just that I've seen other writers lose the bulk of their more legitimate writing assignments when it was discovered that they wrote erotica."

The one drawback to using a pen name is that Simons can't take credit for her erotica on her writing résumé, "so it appears, at the moment, that I have no fiction writing credits." However, adds Simons, "I've received strange 'fan' mail, and I'm just as happy that those people can't easily find me."

■ **Negotiate.** When Diana and her husband were honeymooning in Italy, her husband dropped a bomb on her. He wanted her to keep their personal lives personal: no articles about husbands who stole the covers or snored too loudly, or printed disclosures about how they really met. Diana accused her husband of being a hyp-

---

* This name has been changed. (See, we follow our own advice.)

ocrite … it was okay for everyone else in the United States to have freedom of speech, just not her. Tears were shed, words were exchanged, but over a couple of months they negotiated a compromise. Diana promised that she would never mention her husband by name in any of her articles and that she'd continue writing under her maiden name. And her husband agreed to zip his lips when it came to subjects she wanted to write about. Now that they have a family, at some point, Diana will need to talk to her son about what's off-limits. Until he can start negotiating, all potty training anecdotes are up for grabs.

RULE: It's boring to use "says" all the time. Jazz up your writing with synonyms such as "yelled," "sobbed," and "giggled."

We know one book on the market offers writers 150 synonyms for "said," but we say, "No way." And we don't stutter it, or blurt it, or twang it. We just say it.

We use the verb "say" so much that we tend to gloss right over all the "he saids" and "she saids." Once in a while it's refreshing to use a different verb, but constantly going out of your way to use different verbs in place of "say" jolts the reader from the flow of the writing.

Besides, you can't really "giggle" out a sentence, nor can you "anguish" or "sigh" it, unless you're the heroine of a badly written romance novel.

When Linda interned at a lifestyle magazine in San Francisco, she once edited an article by a writer who apparently had a phobia of the word "say." His sources all snorted, riffed, chuckled, and wheedled, and this made the writing sound amateurish and drew the reader's attention from what was actually being said. Linda went doggedly through the article, changing 99 percent of the writer's unique creations to the plain old boring word "said." Ah, we say, sweet bliss.

RULE: Use perfect grammar.

As a writer, you should know the rules of grammar. Even if you can't explain the rules, you often know in your bones when a verb is in the wrong tense or a word is used incorrectly. But as you become more experienced, you'll learn that sometimes breaking grammar rules makes for stronger copy.

Many of the rules that were drummed into you in elementary school can be safely erased from your memory banks. "A whole bunch of rules were never historically a part of our language," says Howard Faulkner, Ph.D., an English and grammar professor at Washburn University in Topeka, Kansas. "When grammar books started being written in the 1700s, Latin was taken as the model. But Latin is a particularly bad model because it's a synthetic language, meaning it depends on word endings as opposed to word order as in English. So these early grammar books promulgated these 'rules,' and for some reason they keep coming down." For example:

■ **Never split an infinitive.** "Developed by a bunch of stuffed-shirt Latin scholars, our split infinitives don't have the same change to the sentence as it would in Latin," says freelance writer Maggie Bonham. In fact, an infinitive *can't* be split in Latin because it's all one word, so this rule doesn't translate well to English. "The rule is worthless, in my opinion. As one who has studied both Anglo-Saxon and Latin, I can say this!"

"Instinctively, some things sound better with a certain word order," Bohnam continues. "We know that the *to* in the phrase 'to boldly go,' (from Star Trek) works with the infinitive verb 'go.' If we were to correct the split infinitive, I don't think it would make that big of a clarification. Besides, 'To boldly go where no one has gone before,' sounds so much better than 'To go boldly where no one has gone before.' " The bottom line: Use your judgment.

■ **Never start a sentence with 'and' or 'but.'** "If you have a teacher who says this, bring a copy of the Bible into class – the

King James version," says Faulkner. "I'm sure the teacher will say 'This is a masterpiece of literature.' Open it to any page at random, and you will find sentence after sentence beginning with 'and' or 'but.' "

■ **Never end a sentence with a preposition.** Lies, lies, and more lies. "It's perfectly normal and natural to end sentences with a preposition," says Faulkner.

■ **Never use sentence fragments.** For beginning writers, this is a good rule to follow as sentence fragments, used improperly, can confuse the reader. But once you know what you're doing, fragment away! "I have a book coming out in December, and the second paragraph opens with 'Shamefully' – period," says Faulkner. "It was meant to be grammatically effective."

In conclusion: Don't let the grammar books get you down! Learn the rules, but remember that rules can be effectively broken in the hands of a skilled writer – and that some rules, like the ones above, aren't even rules at all.

RULE: You have to hit the word count dead on.

Freelancer Judy Waytiuk is really on the ball. If she gets an assignment for 1,200 words, she hands in 1,200 words. On the dot. Even if she has to add or subtract an adjective or two.

That's great if you can do it, but don't let word-count worries keep you awake at night. We've heard that it's usually okay to miss the word count by plus or minus ten percent. So if you have an assignment for 2,000 words, 1,800 to 2,200 words would technically be acceptable.

However, we must add that most editors we know would be disappointed, if not annoyed, if you handed in a piece that's 200 words too short. Come on, you're a writer! Add words! Over is always better than under, as it's easier for your editor to trim words than to add them.

In fact, many editors *prefer* to receive an article that goes above and beyond the word count. "When an editor specifies word length, you might want to give 200 extra words," says Arnold Howard of *Martial Arts Professional*. "That way the editor can chop deadwood without the article running short. Most articles contain deadwood. Getting rid of it vastly improves the article, but it takes a lot of experience for the writer to find all of it."

But by a "bit" over the word count, we mean 100 or 200 words over – not doubling it! Naturally, if you're writing a 200-word short, we don't advise going 100 or 200 words over the limit. "I hate it when an article comes in double the assigned word count," says Elisa Bosley, senior food editor of *Delicious Living*. "[It's] too much work to cut it down, and it means the writer isn't distilling the important information him or herself – leaving me to do it instead."

But don't let the length constraint keep you from throwing in a few sidebars, even if they take you over the word count. If you have extra information from your research and can whip out a sidebar or two, your editor will love you even more than she already undoubtedly does.

RULE: You should always turn your articles in on time.

Would your editor rather receive a timely piece of junk or a great article that's a few days late? "Neither is good," says Jeremy White, editor of *Pizza Today*, "but a great article a day or two after deadline, provided the writer asked for an extension, is preferable to a sub-par article that will eventually take more time due to the need for re-writing or heavy editing. A sub-par article means the writer probably will not get another assignment. A great article that comes in late will get a new writer one more chance – but the next one better be on time."

Your deadline decision also depends on the situation. If your editor says she's in a rush and needs the article by a certain date or else, you might make her look bad to her superiors if the article isn't ready on time – and we hope by now you've figured out that your job is to make your editors' jobs easier, not extinct. Your delinquent article could even cause the magazine to be late to the printer, which won't endear you to your editor, either. If you're having problems with an article and you can't get a deadline extension, do everything within your power to make your article perfect; pulling an all-nighter and asking writer friends for comments and suggestions are two ways to do this.

You'll probably get a feeling during your research and hunt for sources whether the assignment will be troublesome. If you have an inkling that you're not going to make the deadline, call your editor as soon as possible to ask for an extension rather than submit something that's on time but not your best work.

RULE: Once you've turned the article in, it's out of your hands.

Smart freelancers request to see the galley proofs – a copy of the edited and laid-out article – before the magazine goes to press.

And for good reason. Linda once wrote an article about spring cleaning for a popular women's magazine, turned it in, and promptly forgot about it. What a nasty surprise she had when she saw the article in the magazine – the editors had invented quotes for her sources! We're not talking slightly altered quotes – we're talking completely new and made-up facts and assertions.

Another writer we know (who wishes to remain anonymous) wrote a weight-loss article for one of the biggest health mags in the country. The editors, apparently deciding the quotes weren't juicy enough, had one of the writer's sources say, "I was as fat as a pig." Boy, was the source unhappy when the article hit the stands and he saw the words that had been put into his mouth!

Other mistakes that make it into print may be less galling than the examples above, but they're no less annoying. For example, when Diana got married, one of her editors mistakenly assumed she'd be using her new last name for her byline. But Diana didn't see her new byline until the magazine hit the newsstands. Linda, on the other hand, learned her lesson after her women's magazine debacle. She recently received galleys from a career magazine and found that they had spelled her name wrong in the byline. She called the editor right away and they fixed the embarrassing blooper before it reached print.

The moral of the story: It's always good to have a gander at your article before it goes to press. Not all magazines will let you review the galley proofs of your article, but it never hurts to ask – especially if you've signed a contract where you guarantee that everything contained in the article is true. What happens if one of your editors changes a quote? Can you still guarantee that your article is free from error? Nope, so you should insist that this kind of contract include a clause promising you a look at the article before it goes to the printers.

RULE: They have fact checkers and proofreaders at the magazine to handle that stuff.

If you interviewed the Reverend Doctor Jerzy Sczyzlowski, Ph.D., M.D., R.D., why bother checking and rechecking that you got his name, title, and affiliations right? And if a source gives you a statistic, don't get your pants into a knot double-checking it. After all, that's why magazines have fact checkers – to check your facts. Right?

Well, it's true that the fact checkers are indeed there to check your facts, so if you make a minor screw-up, with their help it might not make its way into print. But believe us, they do work in the same building as the editors, and they do talk. If you commit too many faux pas, your editor will find out, and he'll think that you did a sloppy job on the article. And you know what? He would be right. "Writers should double-check their facts, stats and quotes," says Jeremy White of *Pizza Today*. "That's part of being professional and accountable. If we turn up too many inconsistencies, that tells us the writer rushed through the process and is not worthy of another assignment."

As good business practice, we always double-check our quotes, keep meticulous research notes, and provide our editors with names and phone numbers for our sources. We don't have to be told. "You would never hand in a paper and expect your professor to fact check it – you'd fail," says Nancy LePatourel of *Oxygen*. "Why would you do anything less for your career?"

Besides, fact checkers make mistakes, too. Our names are going to be on these stories, and we're not willing to put our trust into a magazine fact checker or proofreader whose name won't be in 12-point type above the story.

RULE: Never show your article to the source.

Use your discretion. Diana, like many writers, never shows an article to the source before publication. Freelancer Rachel Dickinson has learned to tell sources that she won't share articles before they run. "This sometimes bothers scientists who say I might not get the science right," she says, "but I suspect they're more interested in making sure they sound smart." Linda would never show an article intended for a consumer publication to the source, but when she was starting out she routinely showed completed trade magazine articles to her sources before turning the pieces in to the editor. She often wrote on complicated topics like reprographic printing processes and call center technology and figured that showing the articles to the sources was an easy way to check her facts. The sources were usually very good about pointing out factual errors, and her editors never expressed any concerns about this practice.

This practice did backfire on Linda once. She interviewed a UK-based technology company for an article about new printing technologies. For a week after she sent the article for a pre-publication review, she received early-morning, desperate calls from the company's PR person insisting that Linda give the company more play in the article, change quotes to put the company in a better light, and attribute quotes given by other people to the company's source. By this time, Linda had developed more confidence in her writing abilities, and spurred on by this annoying person, she decided to save time by no longer giving her sources a sneak peek at the article. So be warned – if you regularly show your articles to sources, at some point you will assuredly get an overbearing anal-retentive calling you at all hours.

Whether you should let your source take a gander at the article also depends on the kind of article you're writing. If you're working on a very technical piece about cancer research that's full of facts and stats, showing the article to the source may be the way to go. But if you're covering a heated controversy between two state senators, showing the piece to your sources opens the door to never-ending revisions as each source tries to get the upper hand by changing quotes and arguing over facts.

In any case, *always* check with your editor before sharing a story; some have strict rules against the practice, while others prefer it. "I think it's a good idea," says Elisa Bosley of *Delicious Living*. "That way the source knows his or her words and thoughts are being represented accurately. [It] saves time for the fact checker."

What if your source wants to see the article before you turn it in and this goes against your better judgment or your editor's rules? Tell him that you're not allowed to show him the whole article, but you'll ask the editor whether it's okay to show him his quotes for approval. If your editor gives the thumbs-up, copy and paste the quotes with only as much context as necessary into a new document and send it to the source.

RULE: You need to put your article into proper manuscript format.

One-inch margins, double-spaced body, your name and

address in the upper left corner of the first page, and your last name, article title, and page number in the upper left corner of all following pages. Does anyone actually do all this? Maybe in the days of Ye Olde Post Office, when writers turned in their articles in real, actual dead tree form.

In this age of e-mail, most editors prefer to get their articles digitally as an attached text file or within the body of an e-mail message. If you're going the latter route, your fancy headers, double-spacing, and underlined or italicized titles will be magically transformed into a single-spaced document with no formatting. It's best to start off with the article title, your name, and the word count up top, and the article pasted in below. Many e-mail programs don't process tabs or indents correctly, so separate your paragraphs with an extra line space.

As for articles sent as e-mail attachments, ask your editor how she prefers to receive them. Some editors prefer Word documents (.doc), while others like the article saved as Text (.txt) or Rich Text Format (.rtf). Editors also vary in their formatting preferences – for instance, or one versus two spaces after periods, indents at the beginning of paragraphs versus just a return.

Often, a magazine will have its own style sheet, which is a document that tells the writer how to format and turn in articles. Ask your editor if she has one – she'll probably be impressed that you even know what a style sheet is. If they don't have one, you can do what Diana does and review articles in the publication that are similar in length and style to the one you're writing. Note how the magazine handles things like abbreviations, titles, and attributions, and follow their lead on your final copyedit of the article. Your editor will appreciate the extra effort, and anything you do that pleases an editor has a surprising tendency to translate into more dollars for you.

The Renegade Writer

Getting the Green
Don't Be Shy When It Comes Time To Collect

From hiring lawyers to pitching tents outside their editors' offices, at times writers have to go to ridiculous lengths to get paid. When it comes to cutting checks, magazines sometimes seem to rank their writers — the people who supply the magazine's actual content — below their janitors and their in-house masseuses. Keep reading to find out how to break the rules that keep you from getting the checks you've earned.

RULE: The check is in the mail.

We wince when we finally get an accounts payable person, editor, or publisher on the phone and he uses this cliché on us. Because it's usually shorthand for, "We haven't cut a check, and we have no intention of cutting one for you because you're going to be the last one paid around here, sucka." In many cases, when we finally hear this line, we've already been told that the check is on someone's desk or in the bowels of the computer system or waiting to be signed by the sixth vice president of human development, so by this point, we're fairly confident that no such check is in the mail.

We used to accept what our customers told us, thank them

profusely, hang up, and spend the next fourteen days obsessively checking our mailbox, all the while feeling like we're waiting for the Titanic to arrive. Now we're a bit wiser. When an editor, an accounts payable rep, or the publisher tells Diana to hold tight because the check is in the mail, she holds off on her effusive thanks and instead asks for a check number and the date on the check so that her bookkeeper can watch out for it. (She may be her own bookkeeper, but she's very harsh with herself if the books aren't straight.) If they tell her the check has been cut but not mailed yet, she'll ask that they use FedEx to send it, especially if payment is seriously past due. And if they're within driving distance, she'll even say something like, "I'm so glad my check is ready. I'll be over there at, say, 3 p.m. tomorrow to pick it up." Even if she's not in the neighborhood, chances are she has a trustworthy friend who's willing to pick up the check for her (see p. 146).

RULE: Don't bother the editor – she has nothing to do with you getting paid.

Diana once wrote for a business publication that was habitually slow in paying her. We're talking 60 to 90 days past due, with lots of annoying phone calls, pointed e-mails, and old fashioned begging and pleading with the accounts payable manager before she'd get her check. She'd always been told by other writers to go directly to accounts payable, but in this case, these people were oblivious to her need for money.

One day, Diana met her editor for lunch, an editor with whom she had an excellent working relationship. In fact, during the meal, her editor mentioned that she wished all of her freelancers were as headache-free as Diana. That's when Diana realized she had some leverage. When the editor asked Diana if she had any questions or concerns about the magazine, she responded, "As a matter of fact, I do. Is there anything you can do to help me get paid on time?" As the editor's face reddened with embarrassment,

Diana explained that begging the company for her money distracted her from what she was really good at: writing. The editor was appalled that her magazine was habitually late paying her. When they returned to the office, the editor brought Diana down to accounts payable, introduced her to the person who'd been ignoring Diana's phone calls and e-mails, and asked her to cut a check for all outstanding invoices ASAP. It was a sweet, sweet moment.

The way we see it, the accounts payable department is not interested in who you are or how dependable you are or how much you like puppies and small children. You're only a vendor ID number to them, another bill to be paid. Your editor, on the other hand, has much more at stake, especially if you have good history together. So why not use that relationship to your advantage? When your check is late, appeal to your editor first. Just remember to play nice. When Linda is checkless after 30 days (or whatever the contract's terms are), she e-mails the following note to the editor:

> Dear Lovely Editor:
>   I was checking my logs and noticed that I haven't received a check for my article "Why I Love My Editor," which I turned in six weeks ago. Would you mind checking into this for me? Thanks!
>
> Cheers,
> Linda

That's usually enough to start the payment wheels turning.

RULE: Don't use extreme tactics to get your money or you'll never work for that magazine again.

Do you even *want* to work for a magazine that's dragging its heels to pay you? If a publication is treating you badly, and you've exhausted every reasonable tactic to get a check, we say fire away. What do you care if you piss off the accounting staff or an editor who doesn't care about his writers?

One of the best stories we've heard about a writer using extreme tactics to get paid involved a freelancer named Brett Forrest, who was owed almost $4,000 by *Gear*. He was sick of being told for months and months, "The check is in the mail," so he showed up at *Gear*'s offices with a tent, which he pitched in front of the publisher's office. After a few hours of camping activity and some back and forth between Forrest and the magazine's staff, *Gear* finally produced his money.

When Forrest was on his way out the door, his editor, who was in the last office before the exit, called him in. Forrest says, "He told me, 'Too bad we can't work together anymore. We could have worked something out.' Well, after 70 phone calls, I'm not sure that I could have done any more. He asked me not to tell anyone about what had happened, but I'd already told the *New York Observer*. As I was walking down the street, my cell phone rang and it was the editor. He said, 'I've got to hand it to you, that's what makes a good reporter.' " Forrest admits that he worried whether he was doing the right thing by using such an aggressive tactic to get his money, but he knew he didn't want to work for the magazine again. What's more, he says that the experience has made him more valuable to other editors he's worked with and who've heard the story. "They look at me and think, 'He's the kind of guy who can get me my story. He's not afraid.' "

Linda has never had to pitch a tent to collect a check, but she has used extreme tactics to track down her money. When a Detroit-based newsstand magazine was more than eight months late paying Linda $1,300, she called and e-mailed daily, enlisted the help of a National Writers Union grievance officer, and reported the delinquent magazine to writers' organizations and publications. Still no check.

Desperate, Linda logged onto an online forum she frequents and offered $300 to anyone who would visit the magazine's office in person and demand the check. She immediately got a response from a Detroit native named Lisa who was glad for the chance to make a buck and help out a fellow forum member. Lisa e-mailed the editor to tell him she was stopping by on X date at X time. When she got there, the receptionist had the money waiting for her. Unfortunately, the payment consisted of three checks, two of them post-dated, and one of which bounced – but Linda did get $800 of her payment in the bank before the magazine folded a few weeks later.

Here are a few other tactics to consider:

■ **File a small claims suit.** We're surprised at the number of free-lancers who've told us, "It's not worth going after the publisher." If your letters, e-mails, and phone calls go unanswered, enlist the help of the legal system. Many times, the threat of a small claims suit is enough to push a publisher to cut a check. Every state has its own small claims procedures; call your local small claims court for more information. Be aware, though, that your case may not be heard for months; three claims Diana filed in Massachusetts in October 2002 weren't brought before the court until April 2003. The sooner you file a claim for overdue funds, the less time the publisher has to split town.

■ **Enlist the aid of the National Writers Union.** Linda and Diana haven't had luck with the NWU's grievance division yet, but many other freelancers have. Basically, volunteer union members will contact the errant publication on your behalf and work out a payment agreement. The only hitch is, you have to be a union member to take advantage of this service.

■ **Hold your next article hostage.** Simply tell your editor, "I know this piece is due next week, but I can't afford to work on it until I'm paid for the other work I've done." You're putting your editor in a tough spot – he potentially has a gaping hole in an upcoming issue – but now you've made your headache his headache. Diana did this with a technology magazine that was seriously past due paying her on several articles, and she's glad she did, because she's still waiting for her check. She would have been deeper in the hole had she turned in her assignment.

■ **Report the delinquent publication.** Tattle on the nonpaying magazine to organizations like ASJA and the NWU, and to writers' publications like *WritersWeekly* (see Appendix 7, p. 191, for contact info). Writers' organizations usually alert their members to non-paying markets, and *WritersWeekly* will contact the magazine about your complaint before listing the magazine on its Warnings page.

Product review sites are also a good place to vent. Diana went to Epinions.com and detailed how one publisher was launching a new magazine and soliciting for new writers in local newspapers despite owing her $5,000 for work she did the previous year. Some Epinions members were annoyed that Diana didn't talk about the magazine's value or the quality of the articles, but she felt that potential ad buyers and subscribers – not to mention freelancers – should be aware of the publisher's financial standing.

Even if you follow all these suggestions, you may never be paid, but by sharing information and complaining loudly, at least you can save other writers from the same sad fate.

RULE: If you signed a contract, you can't renegotiate payment for an assignment.

Your editor at *Sewage Monthly* assigned you 1,000 words on trends in sewage management. You've turned in the assignment on time, and she says the article looks great – but the following Thursday, she asks you to interview two other sewage experts, include their quotes in the article, and provide her with two 200-word sidebars. Oh, and can you get this done by Monday morning? You check your contract, but there's no mention of sidebars.

Many freelancers would simply grit their teeth and get to work, complaining to their significant other or their cat about the unfairness of it all. They figure they signed a contract, so the editor has every right to ask for changes. Changes are fine, and as much as we hate to break it to you, so is a complete rewrite. But should you roll over and play Kick Me Harder when an editor asks for more than what was contracted? We say, "No way." If an editor asks for work that's not included in your contract, that means you can — and should — ask for additional compensation.

A good contract will spell out what is expected of the writer. Many magazines will give writers the option of doing a rewrite (or two) before it foists a kill fee on them. One consumer magazine advised Diana ahead of time that they always made writers rewrite their stories, and not to worry — it was just the way their editorial department worked. But sometimes magazines leave things pretty loosey goosey, which spells bad news for newbie freelancers or writers who are uneasy with confrontation.

As part of their efforts to provide exceptional customer service, Diana and Linda often throw in a couple of sidebars with their stories without being asked — and they don't charge for them. Ninety-nine percent of the time, these sidebars take all of five minutes to create because they use leftover research and quotes from their interviews that were important, but didn't fit into the main text.

But some magazine editors can't stop asking for more-more-more, even when you think you've gone above and beyond the written contract. You have several options:

■ **You can do the additional work.**

■ **You can ask for a kill fee.**

■ **You can call your editor and renegotiate the assignment.**

We think the third option is the sanest option. If you're feeling trod upon, figure out how much it will take for you to feel better — and simply ask for it. This conversation doesn't have to be confrontational. Spell out the situation to your editor: "You've asked me to add two 200-word sidebars and include additional research in my article that will bring the word count well above the 1,000 words we agreed upon." Then, present a solution: "I estimate this is an additional 500 words above the assigned amount, plus time for research, so do you agree it's fair to amend the contract for the extra work?" Do this all matter-of-factly, with no tentative, permission-hungry, wishy-washy tone to your voice. If the editor rules out the extra payment, you'll need to decide whether she's a client you can't afford to lose, or a client you can't afford to keep. But either way, at least you've taken action rather than seethed in front of the computer all weekend.

RULE: If your article gets 'killed,' all you can expect is your kill fee.

In many of the contracts that land on your desk, you'll notice a clause that goes something like this: "If the article is deemed unacceptable by the editor after the writer has been given the chance to remedy the situation, then a kill fee of X percent of the contracted amount will be paid to the writer." Kill fees usually run from 10 to 25 percent of the article fee; many freelancers negotiate up to 50 percent. Negotiating a higher kill fee is a lot like making a prenuptial agreement: You plan to knock your editor's socks off with your skill and professionalism, but if this relationship doesn't work out, you want to walk away with as much money in your pocket as you can.

No writer likes having her article killed, but sometimes taking the money you're offered and running feels good, such as when you've done a couple of rewrites on your story and your editor ain't finding satisfaction. You may even broach the subject of the kill fee with her, especially if you know you'll have no trouble finding a new home for the story. Diana once wrote an article for a newly launched golfing magazine. She handed it in to her editor, who soon quit. The article went off to another editor, who also

Chapter 8 - Getting the Green

quit. A third editor came along, who didn't bother to answer Diana's e-mails or telephone calls. Finally, when she heard this editor had also left, Diana saw the writing on the wall and approached the editor-in-chief about getting her kill fee. Within weeks, the money was in her pocket – and a good thing, too, because the magazine shut down soon thereafter.

A good contract will spell out what kind of kill fee will be paid if the article is deemed unacceptable for publication after a certain number of rewrites. The writer can then walk away from the project with a bit of coinage in her pocket, free to sell the story to a more appreciative magazine. But kill fees lean toward the evil end of the moral scale when publishers and editors use them to satisfy their flaky whims. What really sucks is when you've done your work and your editor says she's satisfied with it – but you hear nothing until a month later, when the editor calls and announces chirpily, "We're killing the article because it doesn't fit with our new editor-in-chief's vision. Your kill fee is in the mail."

What, like now you have to be a fortune teller? Can you imagine hiring a contractor to paint your home's interior walls in Williamsburg Blue and Colonial Red, and then telling him when he's finished, "I'm not going to pay you for this work because I was just watching reruns of 'Miami Vice' and now I'm into the South Beach look"? And how would your editor feel if her publisher came up to her in the hallway and said, "Hey, Jane, great work editing those stories we'd planned for the next issue, but since we're going in another direction, we won't be paying your salary for that week." That sums up how many magazines treat their freelancers.

Should this happen to you, first check your contract for the wording, but then request your full fee, explaining that the kill fee covers work that is unsatisfactory, not untimely (at least from the magazine's new and improved perspective). Many editors will agree and go to bat to get you the full fee, or at the very least, a greater percentage of money than the kill fee specified. You won't know until you ask – and unfortunately, many freelancers sit back and wearily accept the kill fee instead of standing ground.

RULE: You will be paid according to your contract's terms.

In good economies and bad, freelancers are usually the last in line to get paid. Magazines know that we writers have little clout compared to the printer or the magazine's staff, so they'll often string us along.

One of Diana's old clients was supposed to pay 60 days after acceptance, but they regularly went to 90 or 120 days, and that was with a lot of badgering, pleading, and finally, threats. The point of this is to warn you, especially if you're new to the freelancing game, that checks seldom appear when they're supposed to, so don't go off and get all jiggy on your credit cards, figuring that a whole wad of checks will appear like magic in your mailbox next week. The most successful freelancers we know have a lot of money in the pipeline, so something's usually coming in, but half the time that cash was due months ago.

RULE: Writers don't need to send invoices.

We've heard this from many an editor: "Don't worry about an invoice; we'll submit the paperwork for you." That's lovely and we thank them profusely for expediting payment, but we still invoice our editors by mail, fax, or e-mail.

Having a basic accounting system will help you tremendously at tax time. It doesn't have to be fancy – a spreadsheet to track expenses and income suffices – and you can easily create an invoice template in a word processing program. Moreover, if you have a lot of checks coming in, or you're doing a lot of work, you can often forget who owes you big bucks and who has paid. A simple accounting system, updated weekly, will keep your business humming along nicely.

Diana successfully worked off a Microsoft Excel spreadsheet and Word invoicing system for a couple of years, but being the software junkie she is, she was lured by clever ad copy into using

Chapter 8 - Getting the Green

QuickBooks. While a wonderful accounting package, QuickBooks was overkill for her needs. So she had her husband help set up business accounts on Quicken, the software program she uses for her everyday finances.

Linda, still living in the Stone Ages, creates her invoices in Microsoft Word and logs them into a notebook with a pen. Hey, it works for her. So no matter what your technological abilities, make sure you have the means to write and track invoices.

The Renegade Writer

Chapter Nine

The Renegade Attitude
Your Success Often Depends On Your Mindset

Successful freelancing is all about banishing bad attitude – the attitude that you're not a rocking writer who deserves the best treatment and pay, that editors are not your buddies, that leads and ideas are meant to be hoarded, not shared. You can easily develop a losing attitude when dealing with reticent sources, ridiculous rewrites, and nonpaying magazines, but if you let this happen, you'll come to hate the writing life. Let the love fly, people!

RULE: It's strictly business.

Contrary to what many writers tell you, editors are not overworked and underpaid gremlins who eat freelancers for breakfast. Okay, a fair number of them *are* overworked and underpaid, but we take issue with the breakfast part (and we're still researching the gremlin issue). We've found that magazine editors are generally an amiable lot – and should you find yourself on the receiving end of lots of assignments from them, don't be surprised if you become friendly with one or two (or more!) editors, especially if you've visited them in person and you're no longer a faceless name who turns in great copy.

Now, before visions of schmoozy, table-hopping meetings at

Tavern on the Green with Jann Wenner and Anna Wintour take over your fantasy life, let's take a reality check. Unless you're a big-name, like Dominick Dunne or Joan Didion or one of the young, hot British imports who occasionally leave their mark on American magazine pages, you'll probably get no closer to Jann or Anna than by reading *Rolling Stone* and *Vogue*.

The reality is that although you may never break bread with the big guys, you can build a friendly relationship with the editors you work with continually. You start out with a lot in common – a love of language and a commitment to the magazine – so usually some kind of personal relationship develops once you start working together.

Diana, for instance, has developed a variety of relationships with her editors. One editor, who's assigned her lots of shorts for two different magazines, has never met with her in person, but their e-mails and telephone calls are friendly, if not chatty. Another editor both Diana and Linda know went freelance, and now they occasionally meet up to "talk shop."

It's hard to work with an editor on article after article and not build a rapport – and why should you prevent a genuine friendship from developing in the name of acting "professional"? Diana strives to keep communications with her editors friendly, yet businesslike, by imagining that they're co-workers sitting on the other side of the building. She wouldn't send co-workers stiff, formal missives, and she also wouldn't forward chain-mail virus warnings or cutesy animated holiday GIFs. (And if you are doing stuff like this now, stop it immediately. Not only are you annoying the hell out of your editors, you're probably annoying the hell out of everyone on your distribution list – they're just not telling you.)

Linda sends her editors Christmas cards, plus congratulation cards when they get married, have a baby, or get a new job or promotion. After all, these are the people who keep her mortgage paid … why not treat them nicely?

Linda's husband Eric lets editors see his funny side. In a list of ideas he sent to his editor at *Woman's Day*, he included, "15 Ways to Achieve Nuclear Détente in Your Neighborhood." Did his editor snap back with a disgusted e-mail? Did she vow to never work with this unprofessional wiseass again? No – she laughed and assigned him another idea off the list. Lastly, Diana, who profoundly misses *Spy Magazine*, created an X-rated version of an article she'd written for an online magazine and sent it to another editor at the same magazine. He liked it so much, he included it on a satirical website he set up with his editor friends.

You don't necessarily have to send gag e-mails to your editors to make them love you. Sometimes you just have to let your hair down, so to speak. Writer Bethanne Kelly Patrick landed a contributing editorship with a newsstand magazine simply by heading off to a comedy club with a bunch of writers and editors. "The editor of the magazine I now work with and I hit it off," she says. "Thank goodness he likes my work, too!"

As a professional (or aspiring) writer, you know not to scrawl your query letters in crayon on cocktail napkins. You know not to start your letters with, "Yo, home girl!" And you know enough to hand in articles that are on time and on target. But don't let your professional demeanor get in the way of establishing friendly relationships with your editors.

RULE: Editors pay your rent, so you should do everything you can to please them.

Most editors you'll meet during your career are pleasant, if not wonderful, guys and gals, but we'd be remiss in our duties as your freelancing buddies if we failed to talk about the editors from hell.

Oy, and we've met a few of them. Some are mere gatekeepers at the entrance of Hades: They forget to forward our invoices to the accounting department, or they take forever to respond to our queries. Then we have Satan's minions – hellacious editors, who put our lives in the lower reaches. They will ask you to write about one thing, then come back and tell you that they need it written *this* way. You turn that in, but, Oh no! It needs a second rewrite, but this time with a little of, oh, I don't know what! (But you are expected to know because you're a mind reader as well as a free-lancer.) A few more rewrites, and then silence before you get the kill fee ... which usually arrives way after your rent was due.

One group of Beelzebub's helpers proved particularly troublesome to us. The lead editor was always tentative and unsure of herself on the telephone, and every other editor felt compelled to stick his pitchfork into every story we turned in until it bled red from a thousand cuts. (Oh, if you haven't been edited by committee yet, you're in for a treat someday.) We banished the troublemakers, and soon better assignments came along to take their place.

If you do run into an editor who's impossible to please, before refusing work from her, you may want to ask what you can do to make her happy. You can say something like, "The last article I wrote for you required so many revisions out of the scope of the original assignment that I had to turn down other work to make the changes. Is there anything we can do to make sure this doesn't happen again?" You can offer to turn in an outline for the editor to approve or suggest that she give you more detailed article descriptions in the future. This demonstrates to the editor that you're willing to put out the effort to make the relationship work. She may give you some good advice and — nice surprise — she may even come to the realization that her way of working is damaging her relationship with her writers.

If that doesn't work, you may have no choice but to "fire" your editor. Don't burn any bridges by handing the editor a pink slip filled with profanities and accusations; instead, when she contacts you with another assignment, either decline the offer with no explanation or answer more directly that although you regret it, you can't write for her anymore because your talents and her magazine don't seem to be a good fit.

You could also raise your rates. Diana did this with a local client who gave her a lot of migraines. One day she was in a meeting with the big boss, a guy who had terminal foot-in-mouth disease, who informed her there were two types of writers — there was a top-tier and there were "others, like you." Ouch! Even this guy's staff members winced. But upon reflection, Diana figured out that top-tier writers commanded more money, especially when they had to deal with PITAs like this. The next time he asked her to quote on a project, she informed him that she'd raised her hourly rate to $85! And you know what? He paid it until he supposedly found "other writers" to take her place.

This tactic can also work for troublesome magazines. Money isn't everything, but sometimes it makes a painful job more bearable.

RULE: Freelance writing is an ultra-competitive field.

Linda asked several of her editors what percentage of the writers they hire turn in good work on time. The answer: 10 percent. Similarly, *Shape* editor Anne Russell says that only 10 percent of the queries that cross her desk warrant serious consideration. She'll pass these queries on to the appropriate editors, but out of those 10%, she guesses that 1% result in an actual assignment.

This is great news that 90 percent of the writers out there pose no competition for you. Unfortunately, the losers who make up that portion of the freelancing population are constantly banging on your editors' doors, making it difficult for even the best writer's voice to rise above the din. And many of these lame-os have impressive clips that are more the result of their editors' hard work than of their own talents, which helps them get a foot in the door while you're still waiting outside. Only after trying – and being unsatisfied with – all those other writers will the editor be ready to give you a try.

Fighting your way through hordes of feeble freelancers is annoying, but you can do little about the situation other than take solace in the fact that if you're part of the 10 percent of writers that editors can depend on, once you finally wedge your foot in the door, your editors will come to you again and again.

RULE: It's okay to wallow in rejection for a little while before moving on.

As professional freelancers, we urge you not to do any kind of professional wallowing, except when you've got a stack of acceptances and checks all around you – then we say wallow in your bounteous wealth with glee. But with rejections? Why bother wallowing for even a second?

We think writers should stop placing so much emphasis on "rejections." They're not rejections – they're business decisions. What if your attorney or massage therapist moped around in their bathrobes like writers do whenever they lost a potential client? Sure, your attorney or massage therapist would be disappointed, but if they are interested in staying in business, they'd simply move on to their next case or look for someone else with painful muscle spasms.

One of the gifts Diana received during her ten years working in advertising and marketing was a thick skin. Not only were her great ideas shot down with regularity, but they were shot down in public, with everyone watching – and sometimes laughing! What hurt more was when they were ignored. But one day she realized that her co-workers and clients weren't laughing at or ignoring *her* – they were laughing at or ignoring her *ideas*. It was nothing she needed to take personally. So when an editor shoots off a note saying, "This idea doesn't work for us," Diana knows it's not half as bad as having copy concepts shot down in person by an unhappy client.

RULE: Writers are always the ones who get screwed.

While you may think that editors have nothing to do but torture writers while they kick back and get footrubs, the reverse is often true. Check out this story from the editor of a restaurant industry trade magazine:

A few years ago, this editor hired a writer to profile a restaurant in California based on the writer's excellent query. The writer dragged his heels on the assignment, but finally turned in a piece that was so good that the editor decided to expand it into a feature.

When the editor tried to contact the owner of the restaurant to verify his quotes, the restaurant couldn't be located. The editor checked the restaurant guide and called California information. Nada.

The editor then tried to contact the several suppliers who were quoted in the article, only to find out that they didn't exist either. The writer had clearly made up the entire article from his fevered imagination. If the editor hadn't been diligent in his fact checking, this fakery would have run in the magazine, embarrassing the editor and the entire magazine staff. When the editor wrote to the writer to find out what the heck was going on, he got no answer – of course.

Similar cases of writers turning fiction into fact include *Boston Globe* columnist Mike Barnacle, who resigned in 1998 amid accusations that he fabricated the characters in a 1995 column, and Stephen Glass, a former staff writer for *The New Republic* who scammed not only his employer, but also *Rolling Stone, George,* and other magazines with articles that included imaginary sources and fabricated quotes.

Imagine how many writers are giving the editors the runaround in their quest to make a buck. Imagine trying to do your job with the stress of knowing that your writers could be screwing you over. Then imagine dealing with prima donna writers who whine over the smallest edits, writers who disappear at deadline time, and writers who can't spell to save their lives. Did we mention that on top of all this, editors have to work in an office with other people – gossipy co-workers and megalomaniacal bosses? And you think doing revisions from the comfort of your home office is bad!

RULE: Don't share leads with other writers.

Diana and Linda met on the 'net. At first, they'd talk about projects they were working on. Then, Diana started writing for a magazine that Linda wrote for regularly, which gave them more common ground. Soon, they were sharing impressions about certain editors, information about who was changing jobs, or advice on what kind of stories Magazine X was looking for. More time passed, and they started giving each other leads or asking if they could use each other's names when approaching new editors.

Around the same time, Linda met another writer – we'll call him Chris – who wanted to query one of the magazines Linda was writing for. Linda gave him insight into the editorial needs of this magazine, and through her editor, Linda heard that Chris had used her name in his introduction letter, which Linda hadn't given him permission to use. Annoying, to say the least. To make things worse, the writer bollixed up the assignment, which didn't make Linda look too good in the eyes of her editor.

Over the next few months, Chris continued to ask Linda for help, and Linda, being the nice person she is, gave it to him. In fact, when Linda developed a closed mailing list for several writer friends for the purpose of sharing leads, she included this person in the group. While everyone else freely shared leads or magazine information, Chris contributed nothing.

Flash forward to the economy bottoming out in 2001. Linda, like many other writers, was finding it hard to place stories, but she heard through the grapevine that Chris had more work than he knew how to handle. So Linda wrote to him and said, "Hey, how about sharing a few names?" Response: silence. Linda never heard from Chris again.

Don't feel sorry for Linda; feel sorry for the tight-fisted writer. Chris learned only to take, not give – not a good strategy for a writer who wants to move ahead with his career. A few other writers on Linda's list noticed the same stingy qualities in this writer, so the group quietly disbanded – only to join forces again without him.

Diana and Linda now have several writer friends that share leads regularly, and they've broken into several magazines using advice from these friends. On the other hand, when Chris hits a slow time – and believe us, he will – who will he turn to for help?

RULE: Be careful – editors will steal your ideas.

In the six years she's been freelancing, Linda has sent hundreds of ideas to magazines – and in only one case does she suspect that an editor stole her idea and gave it to the in-house writing staff. In this case, Linda sent a query to a regional magazine about a Boston man who had an interesting hobby. The editors sent Linda a rejection, saying that they had already assigned that idea to a writer in-house, who had already interviewed her source. But when Linda spoke with the source for another article, he confirmed that he had not been interviewed by the magazine in question – in fact, they hadn't even contacted him yet. Linda feels certain that the editor stole her idea.

But such duplicity is extremely rare. Often, you'll suggest an idea to a magazine, get a rejection slip in the mail, and then, months later, see your very idea in that same magazine. You might suspect the editors stole your idea, but it's more likely that they already had that idea in production when you queried them. With a million freelance writers fighting for page space, duplicate queries happen often. *Shape* editor Anne Russell says, "Right now, I'm seeing five or six pitches a week on yoga. None are unique, but the writers think they are. It's stunning how many writers will come up with the same idea at the same time."

Writers spend far too much time worrying about idea theft. Yes, editors do occasionally steal ideas. Other times, the fates play out so that it looks that way. As Russell says, "Magazines usually have a fairly limited subject area, a narrow focus, so editors have seen every idea under the sun." Why spend so much time worrying about theft? If you feel that someone has played fast and loose with your truly original idea, move on. Make a mental note not to query that editor again. Besides, if this is how she operates, chances are she has other unsavory personal qualities that you'd do best to steer clear of.

RULE: Take every assignment an editor throws your way.

That's okay advice for when you're starting out and desperate for clips and checks, or if you're eager to crack a certain publication. But after awhile, you have to learn to say "No." Sometimes you're busy or you're simply sick of jumping through hoops for a certain editor, so you have to be discriminating.

For example, Linda once wrote for a business magazine that let every editor in the department edit her work. Whenever her articles came back for revisions, they were so covered with red ink that it looked like the editors had sacrificed a goat on them. And many of the remarks were simply ridiculous; when Linda wrote that the color and movement of video displays help attract trade show visitors to your booth, one of the editors commented, "If color and movement attract visitors, why not just have a flashing blue light in your booth?" Yes, this editor seriously expected Linda to address in her 1,000-word article on trade show success why video displays are more effective than a flashing light. Linda gritted her teeth and patiently explained that there's a reason millions of Americans sit fixated in front of their TVs for hours each day – and not in front of a flashing blue light.

After that, Linda refused to take any more assignments from this magazine. Due to all the time she spent on ludicrous revisions, her per-hour rate fell dangerously close to burger-flipping wages. Once she ditched this magazine, she had time to work on getting better assignments from better magazines – and get them she did.

In fact, if you never turn down assignments, you'll never move up in the writing world, because you'll be too busy writing for all the 20-cent-per-word magazines to break into higher-paying ones. When Linda decided after a couple of years that it was time to move up, she (nicely) told the editors at the low-paying trade magazines she wrote for that she couldn't work with them anymore, but that her husband Eric, who was starting out as a freelance writer, would be happy to take on their assignments. This gave Eric a leg up in the freelancing world while giving Linda time to break into better markets.

The Renegade Writer

Chapter

Ten

Thriving, Not Just Surviving
Reach For The Top

Maybe you've already landed assignments, but you can't crack the better-paying magazines. Or maybe you're sick of the feast-or-famine lifestyle of the typical writer. It could be that you're limiting your prospects, not doing the right type of research, or missing out on marketing opportunities. We debunk the common myths that keep you from getting what you want – and what you deserve – from your writing.

RULE: You don't need a website.

Well, having a website isn't imperative; many writers don't, and they do fine. But chew on this – Linda has gotten several assignments from editors who have run across her website, including a biweekly gig that lasted well over a year and netted her $1,400 per month.

Thankfully, you don't have to spend thousands of dollars on a website. You have something that Web designers need – professional writing – and sometimes you can negotiate a barter with them. Linda traded her writing services for a professionally designed site, and then traded services with a different Web designer when she wanted to redesign the site and add special coding. Her site has drawn tons of compliments from editors, and the only cost was her time!

And if you're really brave, you can design the site yourself. Diana created her first, very basic site with a kick-butt software program called Dreamweaver. Dozens of software programs out there will let you create a good-looking site, even if your design skills would give your elementary school art teacher the vapors. Remember, editors aren't going to your site to be wowed by your JavaScripting or animated GIFs; they're there to see your words. Think of your website as your virtual business card; you wouldn't hand an editor a card covered with quills and scrolls and pictures of your six cats, would you? So focus on getting your copy right and making your site easy to navigate, and forget all the digital gew-gaws.

Here's what you can include on your website to wow visiting editors:

■ **A list of published articles.** Linda divided her list into several categories, including health, women's, men's, business, and science/technology. Each article listing includes the article title, the name of the magazine, the article's publication date, and a snappy bit that describes the article topic (usually lifted straight from the article's lead paragraph).

■ **Information on reprints.** Linda marks her articles with a red asterisk as they become available for reprint.

■ **Clips.** You can either link to your articles that appear in online venues or upload the text of the articles yourself, depending on who owns the copyright.

■ **Testimonials.** Linda asks for testimonials from her editors and then includes them on her site.

■ **A photo.** Diana included a picture of herself, so that editors have a face to attach to her name.

If you decide to create your own site, check out other writers' sites and note what you like and don't like about them. You don't have to reinvent the HTML, so to speak, to get the same results on your site. (Once you learn enough HTML to make yourself dangerous, you can browse through the source code – the electronic blueprints – of pages you admire to see how the designer created it.)

If this book inspires you to develop a presence on the Web, be sure to get your own domain name instead of using an address like www.aol.com/members/~writer; it looks a heck of a lot more professional. You'll have to be creative to come up with a name that's not already taken, but don't fall into the trap of being too cutesy. Domains with wordplay like www.thewritestuff.com and www.thewriterink.com are definitely out. Your name – www.jerzysczyzlowski.com – is always a safe bet if all else fails. Still can't find a name? Because of the shortage of catchy domain names, the Internet powers that be came up with seven more Top Level Domains (or TLDs, the last part of the address), including .biz and .info. If you can't find anything in .com or .net, try one of these new TLDs.

RULE: You need to research only the magazine and your assignment topic.

Sure, you need to research those things (though not always; see "Buy six back issues of magazines before querying," p. 55) – but if you truly want to thrive, the research doesn't end there. Smart freelance writers also research their editors.

Plug your editor's name into a search engine and see what pops up. You may find that the editor went to the same small liberal arts college as you, or has a similar hobby, or once lived in the same town. Sometimes, you can even find stuff like transcripts of talks they've made to freelancers in which they specify what kinds of articles they're commissioning. These are all good ice-breakers you can use in your query letter. For example, one of Linda's friends found out that the editor she was pitching a story to liked a certain author. She sent the editor an essay she had written about that same author, and ended up getting a monthly column in the magazine.

RULE: Once you have a full writing schedule, you'll know you've made it.

The temptation to sit back and enjoy the ride will be great, but don't be fooled: No freelance writer, no matter how good she is, can afford to sit back and cool her heels. Nothing lasts forever, including dream editors, lucrative gigs, bull markets, and plum assignments. In just two years Linda lost four regular gigs – weekly project profiles for *SearchCRM* and marketing columns for *1099, Giftware Business,* and *HomeOfficeMag.com.* These losses of regular income (from $250 to $1,400 per month) could have been deadly if Linda hadn't kept the marketing machine humming.

Diana experienced just such a slowdown after going on maternity leave in 2001. When she returned to writing part-time, she felt like she was starting from scratch because the market had changed so much. Unfortunately, when you take a break from marketing yourself, whether it's to procreate your species or to take a six-month trip across Africa, be forewarned that when you return to your computer, you'll need to hustle to get back to where you were when you left. Magazines go belly-up and editors change jobs, so never stop researching new markets. And, ironically, when you're at your busiest is when you need to market yourself the most – otherwise, once you've busted your butt over your current batch of assignments, you'll find yourself with no work at all.

Keep those queries circulating; since it can take months to land an assignment, the time to write queries is *now.* The interviews and research you're doing should be good fodder for more article ideas, so spin off queries from your current work. Even when you're super busy, try to set aside a few hours one day a week to turn out queries. In a couple of months, when all your writing buddies are fretting about their lack of assignments, you'll be glad you put in the effort.

RULE: Writing is the most important thing you do.

Correction: *Marketing* is the most important thing you do. Plenty of talented writers have no work because they don't know how to market themselves. Inversely, tons of sub-par writers get published because they know how to keep their names in front of editors. Remember the editors who told Linda that only 10 percent of published writers actually turn in articles on target and on time? The other 90 percent are mostly mediocre writers with good marketing skills. So imagine what a great writing talent like you could do with the right marketing! Here are tips on marketing yourself:

■ **Keep yourself on your editor's radar.** Every few months, write to all the editors you've worked with to update them on your writing progress and let them know that you'll soon be available for assignments. Linda usually writes:

> Dear Wondrous Editor:
> I hope all's well with you! Things have been going well here – I've recently completed articles for Woman's Day, Men's Fitness, and Oxygen.
> I'm starting to set my assignment schedule for November. Is there anything I can do for you at Blowhard Monthly magazine?
> Thanks, and I look forward to your reply!
>
> Best regards,
> Linda Formichelli

No matter how desperate for work you might actually be, never tell your editors that once your busy period ends, you'll be eating boxed mac and cheese for dinner every night. You want to come across as a successful, in-demand writer, so put a positive spin on your letter.

■ **Take a roadtrip**. Linda and Diana trek to New York City (which, admittedly, is only a 3-hour drive from their homes) to meet with editors for coffee, shoot the bull, and throw around article ideas. They also visit their Boston-based editors when they have the chance. Even if you're busy now, you can make plans to visit editors when the work lets up; set dates, create a travel itinerary, come up with article ideas you can pitch. Even if you get only one article assignment from the trip, that one check will probably more than cover your travel expenses (which are tax deductible in any case).

■ **Surf the Web.** Keep on top of the news in the magazine industry by frequenting such websites as Media Life, Folio, or the American Society of Magazine Editors (see Appendix 9, p. 193). When a new magazine is announced or an editor changes jobs, you can be one of the first to send an introductory letter or query.

There are also fee-paying sites that will keep you updated on publishing news. Diana has subscribed to Freelance Success (www.freelancesuccess.com) for several years; the $89 annual fee deters wannabes, so the members-only bulletin board isn't cluttered with questions like, "What is a query letter?" or "Could someone here give me their editors' names?" The site includes a weekly market guide for publications such as *The Nation*, *Saveur*, *Men's Journal*, and *USA Weekend*. Diana is also a longtime member of The Well, an online community that has literate, intelligent conferences on everything from politics to pop culture. She especially likes the Byline conference for freelance nonfiction writers, which is frequented by writers whose names regularly appear in *The New York Times*, *Vanity Fair*, and *Salon* (the owner of The Well). Often, she'll hear about editors who are leaving or get wind of magazines that are in trouble long before the media find out.

RULE: Your friends and family will be the first to read your stuff.

Diana admits that one of the big perks of the writing life is fantasizing about how the girls who used to taunt her in junior high now gnash their middle-aged molars when they see her byline on newsstands. Okay, we are talking fantasies here. The truth is, Diana's own mom doesn't read her articles, never mind those snarky girls from the Dark Ages of adolescence. (That's why she's admitting this here, because she knows her mother will never read this far into the book. In fact, Diana will probably have to drag her into the bookstore and demand that she look at this book's cover! And once she's seen it, she'll say, "Okay, now that I've looked at your book, let's go look at quilting magazines.")

In fact, only one of Diana's friends shows any deep interest in what she has written, and the rest are politely curious, totally oblivious, or, sadly, mildly jealous. This used to bug Diana, but then she put herself in her friends' shoes. When was the last time she jumped up and down over her college friend's latest successful PR campaign or another friend's much-lauded study of the economic impact of the oil and gas crisis in California? As freelancer Brett Forrest says, "You wouldn't go up to your uncle who works in a factory and say, 'Nice riveting.' As a writer, it would be nice to get that kind of attention, but I don't think it's realistic."

This was a tough lesson for both Linda and Diana. The people you think will be most happy for you may be the most indifferent or oblivious to your successes. Why? Well, who knows? But we're guessing that if they are truly good friends, they're happy for you, just as you're happy for them when they get promoted or land a new job – but they're not going to spaz out for you or ask in a humble tone of voice to touch your hem. Hey, they're your buddies, the people who've listened to you wail about your jerky boyfriends or driven you home when you were too drunk to stand.

On the flip side, your success may indeed stir up envy in friends and family members. After all, when they get a promotion or a new job, it's not as visible as a spread in *The Atlantic*. And how many of your friends and family members honestly love their jobs? Unfortunately, very few people are happy with the work we get paid to do. Even the best of friends can be driven to jealousy when they see someone close to them not only following their dreams but succeeding wildly with them.

So should you tuck your achievements under your hat or wear them proudly on your sleeve? We say do a little of both. We're careful not to gush too effusively about our latest assignments to friends and family members who generally withhold their encouragement. Instead, we save it for those who will get a kick out of our successes. (And if you hang out with people who make you feel really bad about your happiness, then we urge you to find new friends!)

RULE: Magazine writers make their money from magazine writing.

Actually, once you've had success as a magazine writer, you can expand your income by teaching college courses, writing greeting cards, editing textbooks, giving your own seminars, and writing books. You're holding an example of the latter money-maker in your hands right now!

Freelance writer Monique Cuvelier and a business partner earned extra moolah by putting on a writing seminar in Boston. Monique talked about the business aspect of the job – how to find work – and her partner talked about the actual writing process. They also invited an officer of the National Writers Union to talk about contract issues. The seminar was so successful that they're already planning the next one.

Writer Bethanne Kelly Patrick writes "straight-to-the-library" children's nonfiction and curricula. "With shrinking ad pages and magazines closing all over the place," she says, "I believe that branching out is the best revenge. Sure, we all like to have 2,000-word features in the glossies, but some of this education writing

I do is so enjoyable I can't believe that I get paid as much as I do."

Linda once made a few extra bucks by selling a greeting card idea to a card publisher. Companies also exist that buy your short quips and poetry for mugs, T-shirts, buttons, posters, and more. For more information, check out Jenna Glatzer's book *Sell the Fun Stuff: Writers' and Artists' Market Guidelines for Greeting Cards, Posters, Rubber Stamps, T-Shirts, Aprons, Bumper Stickers, Doormats.*

You can even do copywriting for magazines. For example, Diana was hired to write cover lines for a revamped trade magazine. The editorial staff was having a difficult time understanding the publisher's directive, so they needed someone who could look at the magazine with a fresh perspective. After a few issues, the magazine took this fun work in-house, but not before paying Diana a hefty consulting fee!

RULE: You can't do magazine writing *and* business writing.

As a fledgling freelance writer, Linda thought her query for a profile of a young businesswoman would look much more impressive if she printed it on the letterhead she used for her copywriting services. She printed out the query, signed it with a flourish, and dropped it in the mail, confident that her professional stationery would be the detail that clinched the assignment. A few weeks later, Linda received a call from the editor. She loved the idea, but because of the letterhead she suspected that the article subject might be Linda's client. The thought that Linda's article might really be an advertorial (an ad disguised as an article) caused the editor to reject the idea altogether.

A freelancer is someone who acts independently, so it's no surprise that many freelancers feel they have the right to write anything for anyone who flashes them some green – whether it's an article for a religious magazine or an advertorial for a tobacco company. "I write for anybody who will pay me decent money," says freelance writer Jennie Phipps. "That includes consumer mags, trade mags, PR companies, and publications that buy advertorial. I haven't noticed that it made any difference."

Many magazines you see on the newsstand balance the fine line between journalism and advertising. Consider an article on pet health placed conveniently across from an ad for pet food. Or the piece on easy chicken dinners paired with an ad for prepared frozen chicken. Coincidence? Probably not. In light of this chummy relationship between editorial and advertising, why would a magazine editor balk at the thought of a freelancer being involved in both of those fields?

"As the saying goes, the appearance of evil is as bad as the evil itself," replies Tom Bivins, a professor of public relations and communications ethics in the School of Journalism and Communication at the University of Oregon. "Even if it's not a real conflict of interest, if people perceive it to be, then it might as well be." In other words: Life ain't fair. The editor's job is to deliver the best possible information to readers. So if an editor thinks that you're working in the best interest of your clients instead of the magazine's readership – even if this same editor's magazine overflows with "news" about cosmetics and gas grills – then you've got a problem.

Business writing represents a vast opportunity for magazine writers to boost their bottom lines without stepping too far out of their comfort zones. It requires the same level of effort and know-how on the part of the writer. The hard part is ethically balancing copywriting and editorial activities – and convincing editors that your sense of balance is impeccable. For example, you'd be stupid to include information about products created by one of your business writing clients in a magazine article without divulging this relationship to your editor. If he learns on his own that you have a vested interest in this individual or company, you can write off that magazine for good. "If I had someone working on editorial for me and found out he was on the take from one of the companies he was writing about, I'd be real dubious," says editor Brian Alm of *Rental Management*.

Chapter 10 - Thriving, Not Just Surviving

You and I know that you can keep a comfortable gap between church and state, so to speak – but how can you convince editors of this? Follow these tips.

■ **Draw the line.** The best policy is to draw clear boundaries between your business writing and editorial activities. While most editors won't penalize you for being involved in copywriting, they may shun a writer who creates advertising content for companies in the same industry that the magazine covers. "If you've written advertorials for face cream, that doesn't matter [to us]," says Karen Axelton, editor of *Business Start-Ups*. "But if you've written advertorials for franchises – well, we do a lot of coverage on franchise opportunities."

■ **Come clean.** If an editor asks you to write about one of your business clients, Axelton suggests that you let the editor know about this conflict of interest. "You should be up-front if you've done [copywriting] in the same industry," she advises. "We may want to use another writer." You might lose the battle (a single article assignment) but you'll win the war (future assignments from an editor who knows she can trust you).

■ **Don't ask, don't tell.** If the editor doesn't ask whether you've done business writing, and in your mind no conflict of interest comes between your advertorial activities and your assignment for this magazine, keep your lip zipped. "I don't feel it is necessary for a writer to reveal that they write advertorials," says Kim Lisi, managing editor of *HOMEBusiness Journal*.

At some point you'll probably have both a magazine editor and a potential corporate client in the same industry vying for your affection – and then you'll have to choose between them.

Advertorials can pay a heck of a lot better than articles for trade publications and many small- to medium-sized consumer magazines. But the final decision rests on why you write. If you're devoted to the art of putting pen to paper, business writing may not be as satisfying as editorial. If you're just trying to pay the bills, then business writing is right on the money.

RULE: As a freelancer, you've always got to be hustling.

Once editors discover your incredible writing talents, your amazing ability to turn in assignments on time, and the endless depths of your idea well, you'll find yourself spending more time chasing down leads, interviewing sources, and completing those darned assignments. What a problem to have, right? The trouble is that some freelancers find it difficult to slow down. Some even begin to – the horror! – tire of the freelance lifestyle, but they feel compelled to take on more assignments. The stories they're working on don't excite them. Because they've been doing well financially, their expenses may be higher than they were during their early days. There may be a mortgage, or a new baby in the picture. That means increased pressure to keep the moolah flowing in at a fast clip. Soon, the once enthusiastic freelancer turns into a burned-out shell of his former happy self, ripe for a prescription for Prozac.

We feel that if you're freelancing, you might as well take advantage of one of the major benefits the occupation offers – the ability to do *what* you want *when* you want. Yes, marketing yourself is important, but taking care of yourself and not burning out is equally important. People who work for companies other than their own can rarely take a three-hour lunch, bring their kids to a weekday movie matinee, or simply waste an afternoon kicking back with a good book. But you can ... and should!

When Diana started freelancing full-time, she continued to schedule hairdressing appointments on Saturdays. You see, if she scheduled them during her lunch hour at her previous job, she spent what was supposed to be a relaxing, pampering time worrying about sneaking into the office without her evil boss noticing she took an extra six minutes for lunch. Then one day, after she'd gone freelance, as she struggled with her hairdresser to find a mutually convenient time on a Saturday, it dawned on her: She was her own boss now. And this new boss gave her permission on the spot to get her hair done whenever she damn well pleased.

If you feel yourself burning out, make plans *now* to rest your body, mind and soul. Take a vacation or a mini-break. Visit an old friend in another state. Take up a new hobby or revisit an old one. Do anything that gets you out of the office. And if you have a hard time convincing yourself that the world won't fall apart if you step away from the desk, we say you *really* need to walk away.

RULE: Participate in freelance job boards and auctions.

Dozens of freelance project search sites have popped up online in the past couple of years. These services let you do everything from posting your profile to bidding on writing projects. But are these sites, which promise writers an easy way to find gigs, all that and a bag of chips?

Maybe not. According to the *1099* Index (by the now-defunct *1099* magazine), only two percent of freelancers said they have successfully used project boards to find work.

For one thing, tire-kickers love these sites. Tire-kickers are the crappy leads, the prospects who suck your time and knowledge and give you nothing in return. On freelance project boards, any schmoe can pose as an actual hiring company and request your samples, blood type, and first-born son. Diana got e-mails from countless tire-kickers prior to posting her rates on Guru.com. In her opinion, many "buyers" scan the job boards, gather a lot of names, send out a mass e-mail, collect the information they want from freelancers – stuff like hourly rates, quotes on bogus projects – then use the information for purposes other than hiring writers.

Many of the editors who troll these boards are searching for cheap labor, and regrettably the freelancers who participate are only too happy to oblige. Aspiring freelance writers price their goods as if they're Wal-Mart and the other freelancers are competing mom-and-pop operations. For example, one writer on eLance worked on eight projects and earned a total of $470, which works out to less than $60 per project. Not exactly enough to pay the rent.

Aside from projects that lead nowhere, many of the other "job" postings are flat-out scams. One project on a job board offered the ability to "earn a lifelong, continuous RESIDUAL income every time someone makes a local or long-distance phone call, uses a pager, accesses the Internet, orders a product from the Internet, or uses energy in their home or business." And another fine project trumpeted your ability to "WORK YOUR OWN HOURS YOU GIVE YOURSELF A RAISE WHEN YOU DECIDE YOU'VE EARNED ONE! WE CARRY PRODUCT 'ONE OF ITS KIND' NOW YOU CAN MAKE MONEY AND HAVE FUN!" Er … yeah.

That's not to say sweet gigs can't be found on these project boards. Both Linda and Diana have gotten assignments from their listings on Content Exchange, and Linda once got an assignment from an editor who saw her listing on Monster Talent Market (see Appendix 10, p. 194). Just be sure not to rely on these sites for work, and not to spend too much time bidding for jobs and futzing with your listings when you could be writing queries and sending intros to editors – work that offers a much higher rate of return.

RULE: Freelancing is a lonely business.

Your office looks like an explosion at a stationery store. You have plenty of accounts receivable – if only you had time to send out invoices. The word "sleep" has lost all meaning.

Maybe it's time to hire a virtual assistant.

Now, we're not talking about some science fiction, computer animated babe, but a real live non-computer-animated human being who works with you via phone, fax, and e-mail (and who may or may not be a babe).

Now, while it's true that a VA can't bring you coffee – unless you enjoy opening leaky FedEx packages reeking of Sanka – they can do most other office tasks, including writing letters, doing data entry, bookkeeping, scheduling, marketing, updating websites, invoicing, and handling e-mail. Even filing, that most mundane of mundanities, isn't outside the realm of the VA.

In general, VAs work either on a pay-as-you-go plan or on a retainer plan where you pay up front for, say, ten hours per week. The upside to this is that unlike with a real-life assistant, you don't pay for the time she spends doing her nails or yakking on the phone with her boyfriend. Virtual assistants set their own rates and typically charge $25 per hour and up.

Think you're ready to hire a VA? If so, and you don't have friends in administrative positions who are ready to bolt from their cubicles, check out www.ivaa.com, www.assistu.com, or www.staffcentrix.com for directories of VAs who are pining for your business. Visit the VAs' websites to check their background as well as to look for typos, bad grammar, and anything else that tells you that this person shouldn't be writing letters and doing your bookkeeping.

Even if you don't want to − or can't afford to − hire an assistant, you can find people to take over individual tasks that you don't want to handle. Freelancer Julie Sturgeon uses two transcriptionists and hired an assistant to set up interviews with sources. "I send her a bit about the publication, a deadline date, a list of contacts, and a resource sheet that lists her speech to recite when someone answers the phone," Sturgeon says, adding that her part-time assistant carries a cell phone and calendar with her, too. "She calls the contacts whenever she has a spare minute, mostly leaving voicemails and asking these people for good times to interview." The result? Sturgeon claims that by outsourcing appointment setting and tape transcriptions, she can double her workload doing only the stuff she likes to do − and it also impresses her editors.

We know other writers who've hired assistants to handle administrative stuff, like billing, filing and copying, or to take on more meaty tasks like researching story ideas. And these helpers don't have to be professional secretaries or researchers; such work can be done by a smart, organized high school student who's looking for a few bucks. If you hate sending out invoices and playing collections agent, you can contract with billing services to handle that task for you. Is the mess in your office preventing you from doing the best work you can? Hire a professional organizer to help you out. And if you're feeling like you need someone to help you figure out how to reach the next level of success, try hiring a personal coach. (See Appendix 11p. 195.)

RULE: Freelancing is better than working for a company.

Despite our advice to make the leap from employee to business owner, sometimes freelancing sucks. If you're contemplating the freelance life, take off those rosy glasses and read on:

■ **No company health insurance plan.** Most working people take health insurance for granted; not freelancers. Trying to get a health insurance plan when you're a freelancer can be as painful as jabbing yourself in the eye with a pen, repeatedly. Linda and Eric went without insurance for four years, and finally decided to sign up through a writer's union – to the tune of $500 per month. When the rates jumped to $700 per month, they dropped the insurance for several months before finding a better price through their local Chamber of Commerce.

When Diana tried to get an individual policy in her swinging single days, her agent told her to drop the application before the insurance company could reject her. Why? For two reasons: First, he figured that the insurance carrier would reject her because she'd recently recovered from mono (making her an "insurance risk") and second, if she did apply for insurance somewhere else, she'd have to tell them that she'd been denied insurance in the past – a big red flag for insurers. Because she didn't feel comfortable being without health insurance, she took a full-time technical writing job until she got married – and even then, she and her husband took advantage of her health benefits through COBRA until they ran out 18 months later. (COBRA stands for Consolidated Omnibus Budget Reconciliation Act of 1985, a statute that guarantees employees and their families continued insurance coverage for a specified amount of time after their employer-provided group health insurance coverage ends. You should talk to your employer before you quit to find out what kind of coverage is available.)

■ **No company-sponsored retirement plan.** 401(k) plans, where employers often match your retirement contributions, are for employees; if you want to put aside money from retirement, you'll have to set up an IRA (Individual Retirement Account), Keogh, or SEP (Simplified Employee Pension), and remember to contribute to it regularly. No automatic deductions for you!

■ **Higher taxes.** When you're an employee, your employer pays half of your Social Security tax. As a freelancer, you have to cough up the entire 15 percent on your own.

■ **No paid vacation or sick days.** Can't work because you're laid low with the flu? Too bad, you don't get paid. Want to go on vacation for a week or two? Hope you don't mind taking a pay cut, because you don't get those two weeks per year of paid vacation time like your non-freelance brethren.

■ **No office supplies.** When you work for someone else, all those pens and sticky notes are provided by the Office Supply Fairy. When you're freelance, you have to break out a tutu and wings and become your own Fairy. All those supplies – not to mention the computer, printer, fax machine, paper clips, business cards, Internet access, ink cartridges, paper, and long distance service – come from your magic wand. These goodies are tax deductible, but that's small consolation when they used to be free.

■ **No watercooler chitchat.** Unless you've got a setup like Linda and Diana have with their freelancing husbands, forget Friday morning gabfests in the company kitchenette about who got kicked off "Survivor." Even if you hate working in offices, working at home often gets very lonely – so lonely that you can suddenly find yourself down at the local coffee shop making small talk with any warm body who gets within five feet of your chai.

We're not trying to turn anyone off of freelancing – we just think that you should understand the risks before taking the leap. If we didn't manage to find ways past all these negative issues, we'd never have become freelancers. Once you're making a certain level of income, paying the higher premiums for health insurance, doling out your own cash to stock up the home office, and looking for new ways to stay connected are infinitely preferable to working in someone else's gray cubicle (at least in our opinion!).

RULE: Don't quit your day job.

This phrase is a killjoy. If you really want to freelance full-time, you have to make the leap. In fact, in a business climate where job security has largely vanished, you may be better off drumming up your own business than depending on a faceless corporation for your income.

Before making the move to full-time freelancing, make sure you have enough bucks in the bank to survive for three to six months. When Linda decided to leave her part-time office job to freelance full-time, she and her husband salted away enough money to cover three months' worth of expenses.

Brett Forrest says that when he left his fact-checking job at the magazine, his colleagues at *Men's Journal* asked him, "Are you insane?" By the time he'd given his notice, he had written a few features for the magazine, and he'd made inroads with publications like *Rolling Stone*.

Forrest says the first few months were a challenge. He was living in Manhattan's Lower East Side in a rent-by-month/week/day studio that he shared with a bunch of other writer and editor friends. "The floors slanted and there were cigarette burns all over the carpets from past tenants," he said. "We called it 'the Flophouse.'"

He adds, "It is funny and charming to talk about now, but it was a low point for me. The lowest point came when I walked across the street to this Dominican deli to buy a quarter pound of salami – the cheapest meat they had. I counted out my coins and realized I was a nickel short. I didn't have another nickel on me. The woman who worked there said, 'Oh, I see you here all the time. You can pay me back tomorrow. I know you're good for it.' I hoarded that salami for three days. At that time, I was barely even surviving."

But times got better for Forrest. He started lining up two or three assignments every month, generating enough income to move to a new apartment. Today he writes not only for *Rolling Stone*, but also for *Details*, *Spin*, and *The New York Times Magazine*. He recently published a book through Crown Publishing, and he's off to Moscow to report and write for a number of magazines. And he's yet to return to a nine-to-five job.

Roxanne Nelson worked as a nurse when she started out freelancing. But then a car accident in 1996 prevented her from working for six months. "I was forced to really forge ahead with my writing career if I wanted to eat and pay rent," she says. "By the time I was well enough to work, I decided that I couldn't bear the thought of it. It was a little bit of a struggle, but I was determined to be a writer and never work as a nurse again. And I've never returned to nursing."

So don't let the naysayers hold you back. If you have a cushion to fall back on – money in the bank and/or a partner who's willing to support you for a few months – and motivation in spades to make this freelancing life a reality, then go for it! It probably won't be easy, but living off your writing isn't as impossible as others would have you believe.

Appendix 1: Books for Freelance Writers

Write More, Sell More by Robert W. Bly (Writer's Digest Books) – This book is out of print, but you can often find it used. This book has some excellent tips to help you become more productive.

Feminine Wiles: Creative Techniques for Writing Women's Feature Stories That Sell by Donna Elizabeth Boetig (Word Dancer Press) – An excellent book to have on your shelves if you're interested in cracking the women's magazine market.

Queries and Submissions by Thomas Clark (Writer's Digest Books) - This book is out of print, but you may be able to find it used. This was the book Linda used as a bible when she was starting out.

How to Write Irresistible Query Letters by Lisa Collier Cool (F&W Publications, 2002) – This is one of Diana's favorite books, a classic, but it needs to be updated for electronic submissions. Still, much of the advice contained within is very good.

Magazine Writing That Sells by Don McKinney (Writer's Digest Books) – If you can find this book at the library or at a used book sale, grab it. Written by a former *McCall's* and *Saturday Evening Post* editor, the book contains some inspiring stories of well-known freelancers, as well as excellent checklists of what editors are looking for.

Writer's Market (Writer's Digest Books) - Also available in an online subscription at www.writersmarket.com.

Appendix

Appendix 2: Writer's Guidelines

Writer's Market Online (www.writersmarket.com)
Includes searchable databases of markets and guidelines, and a submission tracker. You can either buy a print version of Writer's Market that includes the Web access price, or skip the book and pay a $29.99 per year subscription fee.

Writers Write Writer's Guideline Directory (www.writerswrite.com/guidelines/)

Writers' Guidelines Database (http://writersdatabase.com)

Writing for Dollars Guideline Database (www.writingfordollars.com/Guidelines.cfm)

Appendix 3: Generating Ideas

SRDS Consumer Magazine Advertising Source™
Created for advertising media buyers, this SRDS (Standard
Rate & Data Service) volume provides a wealth of helpful
information about domestic and international consumer magazines. Check with your local library for availability.

Bacon's Newspaper/Magazine Directory
Check with your local library for availability.

Media Kitty (www.mediakitty.com)
This relatively new Las Vegas, Nev.-based site unites media
with public relations professionals in travel and entertainment
industries around the world.

MyDailyPlan-It.com (www.mydailyplan-it.com/holidays-j-
f.htm)
This site lists national holidays that you can turn into timely
queries.

Travelwriters (www.travelwriters.com)
News, press trip announcements, and writer database for travel
writers.

Eurekalert (www.eurekalert.org)
A news service for journalists sponsored by the American
Association for the Advancement of Science.

ProfNet (www.profnet.com)
Sign up for weekly story leads and roundups.

Appendix

Appendix 4: Signing Contracts

American Society of Journalists and Authors
(www.asja.org/cw/cw.php)
Subscribe to the ASJA's contracts watch newsletter (you don't have to be a member). It'll keep you posted on what magazines are offering to writers.

The Authors Guild (www.authorsguild.org)
Their website offers valuable contract advice for books, periodicals, and electronic rights.

National Writers Union (www.nwu.org)
NWU members in good standing can obtain contract advice by sending an e-mail about the contract in question to advice@nwu.org.

Appendix 5: Finding Sources/Doing Research

EBSCOhost®
A database of consumer and trade publications that can be found in most public libraries across the U.S. You may even be able search the database from your home computer! Check with your local public library for availability.

LexisNexis™ by Credit Card (www.lexisnexis.com/credit-card/default.asp)
Search LexisNexis's databases for free and pay only for the articles and documents you view.

Reporter's Desktop (www.reporter.org)
An excellent portal to Web resources for journalists.

SreeTips (www.sreetips.com)
Columbia University professor Sreenath Sreenivasan's "Smarter Surfing" website has lots of tips and strategies to help you do better research on the internet.

Can We Tape? (http://rcfp.org/taping/index.html)
Before you assume anything about taping your telephone interviews, check out what the Reporters Committee for the Freedom of the Press has to say about the taping laws in your state.

ProfNet (www.profnet.com)
Looking for the perfect quote? Post a request for a source, and your mailbox will be flooded with mostly on-target responses. You can also contact experts directly without posting a query.

ExpertClick (www.expertclick.com)
Previously known as yearbook.com, this site puts you in touch with hundreds of experts.

MediaMap (www.mediamap.com)
Another excellent site for finding sources. This one has a Web-based interface, which keeps your e-mail inbox from being flooded.

Appendix 6: Transcription Services

Sometimes other writers are willing to transcribe tapes for you during their down times. Check out places like the Byline conference at The Well (www.thewell.com), MediaBistro's bulletin board (www.mediabistro.com), Freelance Success's bulletin board (www.freelancesuccess.com), or Freelance Online's bulletin board (www.freelanceonline.com). Note that some of these places have a subscription fee.

Appendix 7: Getting Paid

Writer'sWeekly
(http://www.writersweekly.com/warnings/warnings.html)
This site includes a fairly extensive list of publications that have received complaints from writers. You can even submit your own hit parade.

National Writers Union (www.nwu.org)
NWU members in good standing can obtain grievance assistance by sending an e-mail about your efforts to get paid to advice@nwu.org.

Appendix 8: Conferences

Writers & Editors One-on-One (www.magazinewriters.com)
This popular Chicago-based conference attracts freelancers
from all over the country, as well as editors from top magazines. The conference is held every summer, usually in July,
and fills up fast. Application required; limited to 60 partici-
pants.

ASJA Annual Writers Conference (www.asja.org)
Held each spring, this conference gives you a great excuse to
visit New York. Because of its size and the number of atten-
dees, you won't get much (if any) chance to pitch to editors,
but the many talks and presentations are useful — and networking with your fellow writers is always a boon.

Maui Writers Conference (www.mauiwriters.com)
Sponsored by *Writer's Digest*, this conference appeals mostly to
writers of books, nonfiction and fiction. If you're looking to
make that leap, however, this could be the conference for you,
since many top agents and publishers attend each year.

A complete list of conferences for journalists can be found at
http://writing.shawguides.com/journalism/.

Appendix

Appendix 9: Media News

Bacon's (www.bacons.com)
Bacon's main page has links to up-to-the-minute media updates.

Editor & Publisher (www.editorandpublisher.com)
This newsstand magazine and webzine has lots of news about the publishing industry, particularly newspapers.

Folio Magazine (www.foliomag.com)
Magazine industry news.

MediaBistro (www.mediabistro.com)
All types of media news, occasionally announces magazine debuts.

Media Life (http://209.61.190.23)
News about all media, including personnel changes

The New York Post
(http://www.nypost.com/business/kelly.htm)
The comings and goings in the (mostly) New York media world.

Poynter Online (www.poynter.org)
Touts itself as "everything you need to be a better journalist," and we agree. Aimed toward newspaper writers, but there's valuable stuff for magazine journos, too.

The Write News (www.writenews.com)
If you're too busy to check out this frequently updated news site, you can sign up for their free weekly e-newsletter.

Appendix 10: Job Boards

Content Exchange (www.content-exchange.com)
Touted as "the digital marketplace for online content creators and publishers," Content Exchange seems to turn up more viable projects than other sites. We've both found decent paying work though this site.

Craigslist (www.craigslist.com)
It used to be specific to San Francisco, but now craigslist has boards for Boston, Chicago, LA, and host of other U.S. cities. Look for a freelance gig, or post a help-wanted ad for a part-time transcriptionist.

JournalismJobs.com (www.journalismjobs.com)
Also includes internships and fellowships.

MediaBistro (www.mediabistro.com/joblistings)
You have to register to see the job listings, but it's free and worth the time.

Monique's NewsJobs.net (www.newsjobs.net)
Links to hundreds of journalism job sites. Includes articles by experts.

Monster Talent Market (www.monstertalentmarket.com)

Sunoasis (www.sunoasis.com)
This site has tons of full-time and freelance journalism jobs.

Writers Weekly (www.writersweekly.com)
More job listings, updated weekly.

Appendix

Appendix 11: Services for Freelancers

Aquent Financial Services (www.aquentfinancial.com)
Provides debt-free financing and credit/collection services for
small business owners (that's you!). You can invoice through
Aquent and get paid immediately (minus a service fee), and
Aquent takes care of collecting the money from your cus-
tomers.

AssistU (www.assistu.com)
Looking for a virtual assistant to help you get your life in
order? AssistU's Web site has a referral service.

FactChasers (www.factchasers.com)
These three professional journalists have a sideline research
business. Have a question that's stumping you? It may be
worth it to pay someone else to discover the answer.

Insure.com (www.insure.com)
If you need health insurance (or any kind of insurance), this is
a good place to start. Instant quotes, too!

MyBizOffice (www.mybizoffice.com)
Handles invoicing, collections, tax reporting, insurance, retirement programs, and much more for freelancers.

The International Coach Directory (www.findacoach.com)
Search for a personal coach based on your geographic area,
your occupation, or the type of coaching you're looking for.

The Organized Writer (www.organizedwriter.com)
Most successful writers we know are fairly well organized. If
your organization skills need some work, check out Julie
Hood's website. She'll whip you into shape fast.

Appendix 12: Virtual Watercoolers

Freelance Online (www.freelanceonline.com/wwwboard.html)
There are several experts who frequent this board who are happy to give advice. Be sure to search the archives before posting your question.

Freelance Success (www.freelancesuccess.com)
The yearly subscription of $89 is pricey, but it does keep the amateurs and newsgroup rabble-rousers away. You get a weekly market guide, filled with insider information about magazines that mostly pay $1/word and up, and there's a lively bulletin board where you can network and ask questions.

The Well (www.thewell.com)
The Well's Byline conference is home to a lively group of journalists; however, the regulars there don't suffer newbies lightly. Lurk for a while before posting. Membership is $15 per month.

Appendix

Appendix 13: About Our Sources

As a busy attorney **Karen Dove Barr** daily wrote legal pleadings, briefs, and orders which were read by practically nobody, until a classmate at her thirtieth high school reunion asked her to write a monthly question and answer column for a newsletter directed to the apartment management industry. The thrill of having her views read by strangers motivated her to express more of her opinions in writing. Her essays have been published nationally in *Runner's World* and *Dog Fancy*, regionally in *Fifty Something*, *Running Journal*, *Coastal Senior*, and *Georgia Runner*, and in her local newspaper where all her friends help her to improve her writing.

A writer for over 15 years and a magazine freelancer for the past five years, **Lisa Beamer** has had over 400 articles published in national, regional and local magazines such as *FamilyFun*, *Christian Home & School*, *ePregnancy Magazine*, *Home Educator's Family Times*, *Boise Family Magazine*, *Kids Vermont*, and *Pittsburgh Parent*. Her online publishing credits include *Parenting Today's Teen*, *Spirit-Led Writer*, *Writer's Weekly*, *Myria*, and *GeoParent*. Beamer and her husband live in Pittsburgh, PA, where she homeschools the youngest two of their three children.

Greg Blanchette has written on spec and on assignment for almost 20 years. An inveterate self-propelled traveler, his features on sailboat cruising and water travel have appeared in *Cruising World*, *Sea Kayaker*, and *Pacific Yachting*. Essays and articles under his byline have graced newspapers such as the *Globe and Mail* and the *Vancouver Sun*. He lives in the quaint village of Ucluelet, on the Pacific coast of Vancouver Island, British Columbia.

Cynthia Boris has been writing since she was old enough to hold one of those big fat crayons they give you in kindergarten.

She's an entertainment writer with over one hundred articles in print and is the author of three non-fiction books including the *Official Buffy the Vampire Slayer Pop Quiz.*

Sim Carter is a Los Angeles-based writer who's been freelancing for the last five years. Her credits run the gamut from features in major high-paying national magazines like *Parents* to short stories in literary magazines like Purdue University's *Skylark* where the pay is in single copies. Her work can also be found in the *Los Angeles Times Sunday Magazine, Children, Family Life,* and other parenting magazines nationwide.

Iyna Bort Caruso (iynacaruso.com) is a New York-based freelance writer with more than 150 articles to her credit. Her work has appeared in *The New York Times, Washington Post, Country Living,* and *American History,* among dozens of other publications. In addition, Caruso has written award-winning scripts, commercials and marketing campaigns for corporate and small business clients.

Monique Cuvelier has been freelancing since 1994. She has had hundreds of articles published on everything from garage sales to conspiracy theories, and from computers to careers in major national and international publications, including *Family Circle, CFO, Publish, Smart Computing,* and *Psychology Today.* In 1996, Monique founded NewsJobs.Net, a website geared to help writers find work in the technology age. She is the author of *Best Internet Places for Finding Employment,* a practical guide to finding jobs online, and has taught seminars through NewsJobs.Net, Temple University and the American Society of Journalists and Authors on finding work.

Rachel Dickinson of Freeville, NY, writes about nature (especially birds and birding), science, spirituality, and travel. She has written for the *Christian Science Monitor,* the *New Age Journal, New Choices, Audubon,* and many other magazines and newspapers.

Appendix

For the past fifteen years, **Maureen Dixon** has been an advertising copywriter, marketing materials writer, Web writer, and public relations writer for various ad agencies and companies. She also has written freelance articles for local newspapers, including *The San Francisco Chronicle* and the *Pacific Sun*.

Brett Forrest worked at *Sports Illustrated* and *Men's Journal* before ditching it and going freelance. His articles have appeared in *Spin, Salon, Rolling Stone, Details, Maxim, TV Guide*, and the *New York Times Magazine*. He is the author of *Long Bomb: How the XFL Became TV's Biggest Fiasco* (Crown), and is currently working on several book projects in Moscow.

Renee Heiss

Kelly James-Enger escaped from the law in January 1997, leaving behind a career as an attorney to become a fulltime freelance journalist. Since then, her articles have appeared in more than 40 national magazines including *Redbook, Parents, Woman's Day, Family Circle, Self, Shape*, and *Marie Claire*. She's a contributing editor at *The Writer, Oxygen, Complete Woman*, and *For the Bride* magazines, and is the author of *Ready, Aim, Specialize! Create Your Own Writing Specialty and Make More Money* (The Writer Books, 2003).

Mary Kennedy is a licensed forensic psychologist and the author of 28 young adult novels. She has traveled to Hollywood to write entertainment articles for *Tiger Beat Star*, has written travel pieces for the *Christian Science Monitor* and done celebrity profiles for Gannett News Services. She also wrote for local newspapers in North Carolina and for *True Confessions* magazine before she began writing novels.

Seattle-based freelancer **Roxanne Nelson** has written for *Good Housekeeping, Woman's Day, Hemispheres, Scientific American, Family Fun, WebMD, Salon*, and numerous other magazines and websites. She is also the author of five non-fiction books, the most recent of which is *A Parent's Guide to First Aid* (Mars Publishing, 2002).

If you asked **Liz Palmer** what three things she loves most (people excluded), she wouldn't hesitate before saying writing, history and Australiana. It stands to reason then that out of the twenty short stories and articles she has published, both in print and on the web, about 15 revolve around these themes. She currently has a couple of projects underway, including a novel set in the goldfields of Australia and a children's book of a cockatoo's Christmas in Australia. You can contact Liz at palmer19@austarmetro.com.au. She'd love to hear from you.

Bethanne Kelly Patrick is a contributing editor for *Pages* magazine, where she writes on publishing trends and world literature. She contributes frequently to *Health.com* and is *Military.com*'s Military Legends columnist. Her work has appeared in the *Washington Post Book World, Army Times, Episcopal Life, eBay Magazine*, and *Mid-Atlantic Country*.

Jennie L. Phipps publishes a subscription newsletter, Freelance Success, for professional nonfiction writers. She's also a business writer and a regular contributor to *Newsweek Japan, Electronic Media, Bankrate.com, Industry Week,* and *Investor's Business Daily*, as well as *Health Scout News* and *Modern Physician*. She's passionate about old houses and writes about them for *Old-House Journal, Preservation Online,* and *Smart Homeowner*.

Beth Lee Segal was a textile and accessory designer, and sold vintage textiles and textile designs before embarking on her writing career. She writes about interior design, fashion, textiles, relationships, and shopping. She has published short stories and humor essays in literary magazines and newspapers, has written for many design trade magazines and websites, and currently writes the "Room for Improvement" interior design column for the New York City (Tribeca) neighborhood newspaper, the *Downtown Express*.

Appendix

Jane Simons (a.k.a. "Felicity West")

Elissa Sonnenberg is a writer and editor based in Cincinnati, Ohio. An editor at *Cincinnati Magazine*, she has written for *Family Circle, Mothering, The Christian Science Monitor, Preservation, Pregnancy Magazine,* and numerous other publications, both print and online.

Julie Sturgeon is an Indianapolis-based writer with 18 years of professional writing experience. Her résumé covers everything from lifestyle reporter to investigative reporter, sports writer and editor of two business-to-business magazines. She is also the 1998 winner of the *Writer's Digest* magazine feature article contest, and runner-up in that category in 1997. Besides writing, her passions are traveling, Indiana University basketball, and the movie *Braveheart.*

James D. Thwaites started his writing career in the early '90s with a few published poems. Becoming staff writer for a regional magazine kicked his writing to a higher level and allowed him to write for such varied magazines as *NeWest Review, Bridget's Temple Fiction,* and *Canadian Writer's Journal.* He self-published two books and has worked on and managed numerous web pages.

Veteran Canadian writer, journalist, and broadcaster **Judy Waytiuk** moved into freelance writing in 1994 following more than 20 years of newsgathering and writing as a reporter, commentator, documentary writer, researcher, producer, senior news editor, and on-air anchor for newspaper, public radio, and CBC national and regional television. She has had hundreds of feature-length articles published in dozens of publications. She has written for *Chatelaine, The Globe and Mail, The National Post, Toronto Star, HomeMaker's, IE:Money, Profit,* the *New Age Journal, Cottager, Paddler, Inflight* (Canada 3000's airline magazine), *Nature Canada, Explore, Imperial Oil Review, Discover*

Mexico, and *Belize First* magazine. She co-authored a coffee-table book, *Winnipeg: A Prairie Perspective.*

Arline Zatz is an award-winning author of several books, including *Best Hikes With Children in New Jersey, 30 Bicycle Tours in New Jersey, New Jersey's Great Gardens and Arboretums, New Jersey's Special Places,* and *100 Years of the New Jersey Volunteer Conservation Officer.* In addition, her features and photographs appear in numerous magazines and newspapers nationwide, including *Sports Illustrated, The New York Times, New York Daily News, New York Post,* Amtrak's *Arrive* magazine, and *New Jersey Outdoors.* She has been a freelance writer since 1977 since graduating from Rutgers University.

Index

Index

Index

Index